Michael O. Howler

Mar 68

THE TREE OF LIFE

THE TREE OF LIFE

Sexuality and the Growth of Personality

REGINALD TREVETT

P. J. KENEDY & SONS—NEW YORK

NIHIL OBSTAT: DERMITIUS FOGARTY, D.D., L.C.L. CENSOR DEPUTATUS. IMPRIMATUR: H. GIBNEY, VICARIUS GENERALIS. DATUM SOUTHWARCI DIE 29A JULII 1963.

CONTENTS

Introduction

THE SCIENTIFIC and technological developments of our age have brought immense benefits to mankind. A wide range of material things, available hitherto only to the few, are now within the reach of many. Some of these things are undeniably trivial, serving only to give an ephemeral pleasure to their possessor, but many have the potentiality of widening and deepening our experience of life. Books, record players, the radio and television can bring great intellectual and emotional experiences to the people who use them wisely. Technological developments in industry and the home leave more leisure time than ever before. Facilities for distant travel can reveal to us the great human race which lies beyond the confines of our parish or town. Our opportunities for a full life are great, but we barely utilize them. Our horizon is boundless, but we do not see even what lies immediately before us. Our experience could be deep, but we live always in the shallows. Why?

There are many reasons to account for man's failure to develop himself in parallel with his development of his environment. The one to which the late Reg. Trevett has devoted attention in this book has its origin in the scientific method itself. The scientist must observe in a detached manner; he must experiment. To do this he must often remove the object of his experiment from its natural environment and place it on the laboratory bench. In order to observe the influence of one particular factor, he must artificially control the action of other related factors. In this way he obtains an objective picture of the thing he studies. Yet, even with physical systems, he often finds that when he restores the object of his study to its natural environment it behaves differently, because it is now subject to influences which were not present in the laboratory and of which he was unable to take account.

Man himself has not been spared the scientific approach. Nor, indeed, is it right or necessary that he should. The mistake is to think that the scientific method alone is capable of providing a total picture of man. The scientific analysis of man must objectify something which cannot be wholly objectified, for man's experience of himself is a vital part of his existence. There is a subjective awareness of the self which is unique. The importance of this primary awareness in the realm of love, sex and marriage is the burden of Trevett's message in this book. "There comes a moment in the life of the child when he says for the first time, 'I want' instead of '*me* want', a moment when he begins, however obscurely, to be conscious of himself as a subject and to cease to be an object immersed in his physical and mental environments." But this emerging awareness can be prevented from developing in the way it should when the exclusively scientific approach over-emphasizes the objective at the expense of the subjective. What man can learn by observing himself as a thing outside of himself is but one part of self knowledge. He must also look within if he is to achieve full knowledge of himself.

The ill effects of this neglect of the subjective can be seen in the interpersonal relationships of marriage. The objective approach to housing, furnishing, budgeting, sex and children produces a mechanistic atmosphere which lacks all spirit. All the technique in the world will not compensate for a lack of awareness of self and the spouse as something more than physical organisms which must be operated in a certain way in order to produce the correct response. "The body is something we *are*, not something we *have*. . . . We are back with the mystery of the being we call 'I'."

The worst effects of this aproach are seen in the field of contraception. The body is no longer me; it is an object outside of myself which I modify by chemical or mechanical means so that it will not fulfil the function for which it was originally designed, but will simply serve to give pleasure. But the body is me and I must give myself totally, or, when love demands it, withold myself as in the practice of periodic continence. I must not divorce the body from the soul; I must not use the body as a means; for the body is myself. I am a totality of body and spirit; to divorce the one from the other results in something less than human, something that lacks total awareness of the self.

Reg. Trevett in this his last book gives us a glimpse of things which are beyond the comprehension of those who can see man as nothing more than a mechanism—complex it is true, but still nothing more than a mechanism. By deepening our awareness of the self we shall understand others more fully; not by subjecting them to mensuration in a laboratory, nor by operating upon them in an experimental fashion, but by a reciprocal sharing with them of our primary consciousness of ourselves.　　　　　　　　　　　JOHN MARSHALL,
Institute of Neurology.

I

Subject and Object:
Relationship

IT WOULD seem that there are sufficient books on sex and marriage and that in the spheres of ethics, sociology and theology at least, little or nothing remains to be said. Biologists and psychologists may make further discoveries bearing on sexual problems, sociologists may collect further data and so modify conclusions now established concerning sexual behaviour in general and marriage customs in particular, but the chief problems are well enough known and solutions proposed and acted on with results obvious if not acceptable to us all. Any book upon the subject, it may be felt, can only underline one or other of the conflicting views already held. It is wiser to leave the biologists, psychologists and sociologists to pursue their specialized researches and not attempt to add one more voice to the chorus of those who imagine themselves capable of still further variations on so well-worn a theme.

The fact that this book has been written proves that I do not hold this opinion, and for the following reason. It is a commonplace of experience that logical argument, however cogent in itself, does not necessarily convince, and that an abstract or scientific approach to matters of intensely personal moment seems singularly remote from the realities in question. This is especially the case in regard to sex and marriage. The most painstaking, complete and accurate account of the biological facts of sexuality and the reproductive processes, excellent though it may be as a piece of scientific description, appears to have little or no relation to the experience of falling in love. The most documented psychological inquiry into the role of sexuality in the development of psychic life may seem painfully academic to a married couple struggling to bring up their children and to maintain the love which first brought them together as man and wife. Here, as in all vital experience, scientific description and analysis, philosophical meditation and ethical principles appear to belong to a realm remote from real life. Their account of the whole business lacks precision and immediacy. The here and now situations in which sexuality involves us are all but unrecognizable in the more or less abstract terms of the descriptive, analytical and speculative sciences. We admit that these disciplines bring us information, but information apparently divorced from personal, vital experience.

In the field of ethics the most incontrovertible principles seem little more than external regulations imposed upon an essentially anarchic instinct. We may be prepared to admit the necessity of having principles, but we cannot help viewing them as, at the worst, artificial prohibitions or, at the best, an effort of the mind to control the tempestuous and chaotic vitality of instinctive life. When the theologian insists that the primary end of marriage is the procreation and education of children, we may agree or disagree. In either case we feel that he is speaking in a language of abstraction while we are living in a world of concrete realities where ends and means jostle one another in a confusion which no theological formulation can disentangle. The mind, in short, seems to live in one sphere and the body in another.

This apparent division of spirit and flesh—using the words in their common acceptation—is responsible for many of our difficulties about sexuality. One of the basic assumptions of this book is that this division is not an objective fact but an imaginary dichotomy due to a fundamental, if understandable, bias in Western habits of thought. Galileo's ambition was to measure all that is measurable and to make measurable what is not. This aim has remained the charter of Western science at least until recent years. On the other hand, Newman wrote that he was conscious of only two realities whose existence was absolutely certain—God and himself. These two attitudes to reality represent the real and profound dichotomy in the soul of Western man. It is not, we believe, a dichotomy of soul and body but of subject and object. To use a rough generalization, Western man has learned to be conscious of himself as an object, as something "out there", to be studied, analysed, experimented upon, conquered and used, philosophized about, even explained away. Pope's dictum "the proper study of mankind is man" has been interpreted as an invitation to an objective, scientific, descriptive approach to the mystery of human nature. In contrast to this habit of mind is that of the East. Eastern man, we are told, is conscious primarily of himself and of the universe as one subject which experiences, grows and attains to increasingly higher degrees of consciousness and self-awareness. Some interpretations of Eastern thought appear to abolish all objectivity.

Both these attitudes have their dangers. The Western scientific approach to reality when taken to its furthest point of development leads to the virtual abolition of both subject and object. Certain contemporary thinkers hold that all individual beings, including men, are no more than so many series of events.

These preliminary considerations may seem far removed from the problem of sex and marriage. I believe, however, that they have a direct and immediate bearing upon them, for the whole philosophy of subject and object is of vital importance in the consideration of the married relationship under all its aspects.

Two of the fundamental questions which any inquiry into the status of man in the universe poses from the outset are

"What is consciousness?" and "How does consciousness operate?"

It is necessary, I believe, to make a distinction between primary consciousness and that mediate and indirect consciousness which I shall term secondary. By primary consciousness is meant awareness of ourselves as distinct from other beings, and our awareness of all that we experience directly and of the fact that we observe others also undergoing this very primary experience. By secondary consciousness we are aware of those segments of being, including our own, of which we learn by experiment or information. All scientific knowledge, it is clear, is in the sphere of this type of consciousness.

At this point we may well ask what we *are* directly conscious of. Our Western objective habit tends to keep our consciousness in the shallows of secondary awareness even in relation to ourselves. It is only too easy to fall into the trap and consider ourselves to be that outward appearance and attitude which others see in us, to identify, in Jungian terms, our Persona and our personality. Our own inner life then sinks into the unconscious where it may produce upheavals which become evident in the disguised symbolic form of neurotic symptoms. To say that our consciousness is primarily orientated to our inner life is a doctrine that may seem offensive to scientific ears. Yet if the distinction between primary and secondary consciousness is valid, this doctrine is true. If the primordial fact of which I am aware is that others and myself are distinct entities, which are yet mysteriously linked in the realm of consciousness, then the primary experience of awareness is that of self-consciousness. There comes a moment in the life of the child when he says for the first time, "I want" instead of "*me* want", a moment when he begins, however obscurely, to be conscious of himself as a subject and to cease to be an object immersed in his physical and mental environment.

Our Western poets and artists often speak of recapturing

the childhood vision of the world. This surely is because our preoccupation with the objective, with the realm of secondary consciousness, however fruitful in the spheres of knowledge and practice, has prevented the development of the subjective, primary consciousness. The child's vision of the world as he experiences it at the moment when its external presence makes him realize his own selfhood should grow increasingly deeper and broader. In the modern West it has largely been suppressed in favour of the view of the world as an object to be measured, dissected, explored and exploited.

I am not attempting to deny the validity of scientific explanation but merely to provide pointers to the assessment of its limits in the light of the experienced facts of human consciousness. It may well be that the future will see a synthesis between objective and subjective knowledge, between knowledge derived from active experiment and knowledge developed by the art of contemplation. It is of the first importance that this art should be learned anew, that we should relive that primary immediate relation of subject to subject. Newman's motto was *Cor ad cor loquitur*. These four words— "heart speaks to heart"—express precisely the real relationship of person to person. They also proclaim the essence of our relation to all that is.

Books on marriage, with some notable exceptions, seem to lay too much emphasis on the objective facts of sex and too little upon the equally important subjective factors. In this essay I have tried to do something to redress the balance. The objective facts are taken into account, but for what they are— products of the secondary consciousness. My main purpose has been to explore some at least of the data of the primary consciousness, to contemplate sexuality as present to our immediate awareness in our unfolding experience from infancy to old age.

The facts of relationship are extremely complex and mysterious. From certain points of view it seems to be true that man's being is based on his relationships, that he is a relational and not an absolute being. Three stages in relationship, three degrees they were called by the French philosopher Ledoux, have been described and these can be found exemplified in love. Indeed, no account of human relations can neglect the mystery of love.

The *first degree* is that of early childhood, when we are so immersed in our environment that we cannot properly be said to love. Later, when we move into the centre of our own consciousness, we are tempted to desire the "other" for what it can give and, if we become fixed at this *second degree*, our love will remain self-seeking. Once we are conscious of ourselves we face the mystery of our relation to ourself. If our love is entirely self-regarding, if we are the centre of the universe, if things and persons remain nothing but objects for us, then we refuse to enter the mystery of selfhood. In so far as we grasp but never give, rule but never serve, we not only objectivize others, we also objectivize ourselves. Healthy love of self can never exist unless it arises from and remains rooted in love of others. Our being and personality is bound up with those of others. Love, too, is the fruit of the *third degree* of relation.

Love has been called the giving of oneself to another. We may well ask: how can we give ourselves. We are familiar with the gift of property. We offer presents as a sign of love. When we give time or attention, we turn from our own immediate interests, we submit ourselves to the needs of others. Such sacrifice may culminate in that of life itself. It is here that we reach the heart of the mystery of love, for although we speak of giving life for others, we know that we do not possess life absolutely, we do not even hold it in fee simple. How can we "give" it otherwise than by parenthood? What then is meant by such words as "Greater love hath no man than this, that he gives his life for his friends"?

A woman in travail will choose to die so that her child may

live, a soldier will go to certain death to rescue a comrade. In what sense have they given their lives? Men who do not believe in immortality have offered their lives for others. Whether the personality continues to exist or not, the sacrifice of life involves severance from all the relationships we have known in this life and according to the mode of our existence on earth. The dead mother and the dead soldier have made the supreme act of love. They have gathered up all their own subjective being into one utter and final gesture through which they make themselves the object by whose removal another person may attain or keep his own subjective existence in this world. Thus in them the union of subject and object is complete. In them, love and death are one.

All love, then, is under the sign of sacrifice. But the signs and symbols of our self-giving are not confined to the physical acts of sacrifice. There are sacrifices which are symbolized by attitudes of mind. We speak of mutual tolerance, give-and-take, seeing the other's point of view. All such acts of mutual subjection help to transform the I-Thou relationship into a We-community. When a man declares that he gives himself to a woman he loves, if he really loves her he is stating the plain truth. Although human love is conditioned by our creaturely, limited being, it is nonetheless real, and to give oneself to the uttermost to a fellow human being is to reach the highest degree of relationship of which we are capable, a degree at which there is not only perfect union with the "other" but perfect integration of the self.

By the very fact of our human nature sexuality is destined to be not merely the inevitable evolution of an instinct but the sign and symbol of a spiritual value. The problems which our sex life presents may make us forget this primordial fact. I remember a lecture on sex instruction given by the head of a University Education Department. We were advised to tell adolescents that sex was one of our animal functions which ought to come into full play at puberty, but sociological pressures prevented this and so we had to do the best we could to keep it under control or forget about it until marriage. This attitude can arise from too objective a view of the whole business. The scientific investigation of the sex processes has provided valuable information and shown that throughout the world reproduction of living things has a basic mechanism which is the same in them all. At the same time, it has revealed that the importance of sexuality to the individual and the species increases as we ascend the scale of evolution. As organisms become increasingly complex, so sexuality becomes less and less of a temporary function and develops into a force which pervades the whole body and marks male and female with distinctive primary and secondary characteristics. In the mammalian genus gestation in the womb is followed by lactation, which prolongs the period of dependence on the mother. In most other classes of living beings—the birds are the chief exception—the individual is immediately absorbed at birth into the life of the species as a whole. The new individual in the mammalian genus is cushioned for a time against the pressure of the species. In the case of the human race this is of primary importance as it largely determines for good or ill the psychological traits which exert so profound an influence on adult adjustment to life.

Facts such as these may, however, blind us to the striking differences that exist between man and the other mammals. If we neglect the reality of consciousness we may—like the lecturer—think of sexuality as a purely animal phenomenon in all creatures including ourselves. The evolutionary doctrine of sexual customs, taboos, regulations, ethics as the outcome of a battle against anarchic instinct, will then find willing ears. We may view the sexual history of mankind as a communitarian effort to preserve a mastery over vital forces which, if let loose, would drag us back to lower levels in the evolutionary scale, and thus give a paramount place to sociology in the sexual sphere. We investigate the techniques by means of which the community imposes a sexual code upon the individual and hope in this way to assess the real place of sex in our personal and corporate life.

Indeed any doctrine of sexuality wholly based on the facts of scientific discovery and the theory of evolution will be inadequate to describe the total reality we are considering. The evolutionary theory is inevitably an interpretation of observed facts. It is a product of the secondary consciousness and conditioned by the scientific quest for laws of explanation. This is as it should be. The validity of the theory is not denied by insisting on its limitations. We have simply to avoid projecting on to our consciousness of our own sexuality a form of explanation which operates in another field. To do so is both to reduce the theory itself to the status of a myth and to bar the way to that increase of self-awareness which it is the purpose of this essay to promote.

No book on sex can neglect the great changes which have been wrought in its theory by modern dynamic psychology. I have neither space nor competence to deal with them here. In the context of what has already been said only one point needs to be considered at this stage. If the physical sciences are rooted in the secondary consciousness, psychology, it may be claimed, enters the realm of the primary consciousness and by bringing to our awareness hidden contents of our own inner experience, effects a union of objective and subjective knowledge which is of the highest importance. Jung even seems to suggest that for modern Western man depth analysis plays a part similar to that of contemplation in the psyche of the oriental. Indeed the concept of the unconscious is probably the most vital contribution that psychology has made to our knowledge. Jung in fact is trying to call up all the hidden forces of the psyche to produce that marriage of the I and Thou which achieves the third degree of relation in which subject and object are one. To the extent that psychological considerations are included in the second part of this book I shall inevitably incline towards Jung's subjective view rather than towards Freud's more objective theories, since it is the former which appears to me to be more akin to that quest of subjectivity and inter-subjectivity which I hold to be essential for any valid interpretation of the role of sexuality in the life of men.

II

Childhood

THIS CHAPTER attempts to give a subjective[1] description of
sexual experience during childhood. In the case of infancy,
the task is almost impossible since we have no memory of our
earliest years; almost all we know of infant behaviour is the
result of our observation of others. In recent times, however,
another source of information has been discovered in the
buried emotions bound up with infantile sexuality which
form the complexes investigated by the psychologist. The
neurotic symptoms, physical and mental, the anxiety and
guilt states through which the complexes disturb the primary
consciousness of the adult, the symbolic events that give pattern and meaning, however obscure, to our dreams, all these
may be analysed and made to reveal something of our infantile
sexuality and bring back to some small extent the long-for-
gotten experiences of early childhood. We know that we were
conceived and carried in our mother's womb and that most of
us came to the light of day through the vagina. We have no
recollection of these primordial experiences, although the
psychologist may produce evidence to prove that they continue to have profound influence upon our emotional life.

There are cases of specifically sexual experience in infancy
and childhood. The child with its wholly objective attitude to

---

[1] *Subjective* is here used in its primary sense as that which is related to the
thinking subject, having its source in the mind and, in the widest sense,
belonging to the conscious life.

reality may manipulate its sex organs and develop a precocious interest in them, even though the recollection of such experience soon fades. In any case, the infant's life revolves largely around the fixed points of feeding, evacuation and sleep. Its feeding brings it into contact with the mother's breasts, evacuation draws attention to the genital organs. In a passive, if not in an active sense, much of its life is involved in the external manifestation of its mother's and its own sexuality. Freud was surely right in teaching that these early events must have a determining effect upon the whole of our subsequent sexual life. We may question the hypotheses he constructed upon the facts we cannot deny the conditioning which the facts produce.

The study of the psychological maladjustments of children deprived temporarily or permanently of the love and care of the mother has shown that the general development of the emotions and even of the intellect depends in large part upon a happy and lasting relation of love between child and mother. It is obvious that sexual development will also be influenced by this relation. If sexuality is to lead to a truly adult relation between men and women, any upbringing, even at the earliest stages, which drives the child into an attitude of fear on the one hand or of excessive self-assertion on the other will make the passage to genuine adult status difficult and in many cases impossible. It is generally agreed, for instance, that to encourage too much dependence upon the mother, to allow the child to submerge itself within the mother's personality, may be to prepare the way for homosexual deviations. The mother may easily mistake her spoiling of the child for love. She must learn that love for the child means respecting its own personality and refusing to envelop it in her own. On the other hand, neglect or exaggerated severity will favour the growth of a withdrawal from relationship with others and the sexual urges may turn inwards and lead to masturbation, fantasies and refusal to face the creative tasks of life.

The position of the only child raises difficulties here. The cosmic creative force, of which our sexuality is a manifestation, is so vast in power and range that if it is concentrated upon one child alone the burdens thrust upon him are too great. Not only does he lack companions of his own generation in his own home and within his own relationship to his parents, but he has to absorb the full flood of the combined love of the latter for him, together with all the conscious and unconscious contents of that affection. He is too deeply involved in the relationship of man and wife. Where there are several children, the situation is quite different. The problems and the mysteries of human relations are present in an acute and inescapable form in the large family and have to be solved and lived through if the family is to survive. In the case of the one-child family, the principal problems remain those of husband and wife and it is in these that the child is enveloped. For him as a new person these are problems of the past and he risks isolation from persons of his own status and generation. The effect of this upon his developing sexuality will be obvious.

The education of the child before school age will in fact largely determine its own attitude to others in later life and the degree of sexual maturity to which it will ultimately attain. That the relation of mother and child in these early years is of primary importance is a truism, and although we are aware today of its permanent consequences we may not realize the equally important results upon the child of the relation between husband and wife. The obvious physical aspects of the rearing process—feeding, teaching the child to feed itself, instruction in personal hygiene, encouraging it to play—all these have been proved to contribute far more than was formerly thought to the growth of the personality. These we may leave to one side, and point out the influence of the husband-wife relationship upon the child during this period of essential training. Immediately before and after childbirth, the husband must abstain from intercourse. His reaction to this demand is crucial for the child's welfare. If he meets it in a spirit of impatience and causes anxiety in the wife, there may be unfortunate repercussions even at the purely physical level. Breast-feeding requires physical and mental stability in the mother if the bodily and psychological growth of the baby is to proceed smoothly.

At the weaning stage inter-parental relations take on a new character as far as the child is concerned, especially if he is the first one. Does his presence destroy or lessen the love of the father and mother for each other? Will they draw away from one another as lovers and give all their attention to the new person at the cost of their own mutual love and its sexual expression? On the other hand, the husband may withdraw as far as he is able from the mother-child community and seek comfort elsewhere, in distractions either legitimate or questionable on moral grounds. But is any distraction, any more or less complete withdrawal of the father, legitimate in this situation? If the child is not present in the mutual love of man and wife, if the husband thinks he is justified in leaving the early education of the child entirely to his wife, may she not justifiably claim that she has an equal right to consider the child as extraneous to her relations with her husband? By what authority does he demand that she should devote herself to the child's physical, mental and spiritual welfare, while he refuses to bother himself directly with them? When sexual intercourse is resumed, she will find she is torn between her love for her husband and her love for the child. She senses that, for her husband, intercourse is a means he uses to win her back to himself, now that a third person appears to threaten the complete intimacy and union of the past.

The father may, however, co-operate fully in the upbringing of the child, only to find that his own ideas on education are at variance with those of his wife. This is not a bad thing. It offers an opportunity for genuine love to find a way to reconcile different views. It also raises the possibility of divided counsels which may lead to real enmity and so deprive the child of that security without which it can so easily become the victim of unconscious conflict even at this early stage. The mutual love of the parents here meets a great challenge. If there is true, vital, unselfish intercourse there may ensue a genuine slackening of tension. The physical union, by a law of reciprocal causality, makes it easier for a compromise to be reached; this may well be the best solution from the child's point of view, since it results from self-sacrifice on the part of both his parents, and his interests will have led them to deeper union, in which he will have unconsciously played a major part.

There remains a further possibility. The mother may allow herself to be dominated by the unconscious and therefore un-recognized urge to identify herself with what Jung calls the Great Mother archetype. She will then adopt a possessive attitude towards her child. This will have profound and dis-astrous results on the lives of all three persons involved, although these may not all become apparent until later. Some will be immediate. The man will be baffled by the transforma-tion of the gentle creature he married into this devouring woman. He may experience so acute a revulsion that genuine sexual relations becomes difficult, if not impossible. The great world-religions have seen this danger and have invented sym-bolic ceremonies to counteract the unconscious urge. The most obvious examples in Western cultures are the presentation of the first-born to God in the Temple and the baptismal ritual of the Christian Church. If these sacramental rites are fully understood and lived through rather than accepted as conven-tional gestures, the mother will be purged of the archetypal image. She will be made conscious of the difference between absolute motherhood which—paradoxical though it may sound—is the prerogative of God the Creator and the relative, sacrificial motherhood of the creature. The veneration of

Mary, the mother of God the Son, also helps to overcome the archetypal fixation.

The theory of relationship we have outlined in a previous chapter casts light on the situations we have just discussed. The child must begin its journey through life at the first degree of relation. He must be firmly and solidly embraced in the womb of his parents' love for one another. To deny him this is to thrust him into the second degree, the objective status of consciousness, before he is ready for it. Hence the immense bewilderment which is found in infants who are deprived of parental love, a bewilderment which is translated into physical and mental behaviour that both signify and increase the profound psychological disturbances at work within them.

The first major crisis in the developing consciousness of the child from a normal and undisturbed background occurs with dramatic suddenness when it first goes to school. The school has been so essential an element in the life of Western society that we have to make an effort of will and attention if we are to be aware of its vital influence on the relational situation of both parents and children. It is true, probably, that few of us can remember with any clarity the first periods of our school life. A thorough survey of reminiscences dating from that time would be of value in assessing the effect of the change from home to school life. If this research were to confirm my own experience and it were shown that few adults recollect more than one or two isolated incidents, I should feel justified in claiming that entry into school life is a severance from the home so painful that most of us have repressed our memories of it with such success that they hardly impinge upon our present consciousness. Here I can do little more than mention three of the major issues involved: the impact of the larger social group upon the child; the learning of the techniques of reading and writing; the problem of social class as the child meets it in the classroom. At first sight such experiences seem to have no connection with the growth of sexuality.

But if my contention is true, and sexuality in the human race is linked to the development of consciousness and the successful passage to the third degree of relation, then the web of relationships in which the child is caught is profoundly significant for his sexual life.

In a sense, the sudden transfer of the child to the more public life of the school is similar to his earlier emergence from the womb. The home is a womblike place for the infant. At school, he is either separated from it completely or for long periods each day. The newly born child is not conscious of its own activity, although it makes independent, individual physical movements. There is unconscious activity in the classroom also. The child tends to immerse himself in the collective situation and loses much of the feeling of separate, personal existence. He has also to adjust himself to a new figure of authority. The teacher takes the place of the parents. The child's reaction to this new and immensely significant person will have deep and sometimes permanent effects upon his whole attitude to the world outside the home. As in the case of all crisis situations, this relationship will offer great possibilities and grave dangers. A child who is naturally extroverted may become introverted under the impact of a teacher with whom he cannot live on friendly terms. His physical orientation will be distorted and his mental activity harnessed to an attitude contrary to his inborn character and psychological predispositions. If, on the other hand, a genuinely co-operative relation is formed, he will have taken one of the most valuable steps in his life's journey, since he will have learned to extend the scope of his relations with adults and so have entered on a new and all but infinite field of human inter-subjectivity. The teacher opens or closes the door by which the child enters or remains shut off from the existence of the community at large. And it is in the larger society that he will later establish his own sexuality and be ready to choose his own partner in marriage. The success or failure of his own future existence as father or mother depends, therefore, to some extent at least, upon the pupil-teacher relationship.

Teachers may protest that here I am laying too great a burden upon their shoulders. They have daily to face a classroom full of children. They cannot hope to understand the needs of each one of them. They are bound to leave much to chance and to the general influence of the school as a community. This is true enough and raises the thorny question of parent-teacher co-operation. It is worth noting that medical practice has changed a great deal of late in a similar situation. The children's ward in the hospital was formerly almost out of bounds for parents. Nowadays, the latter are frequently invited to come to it as often as they can and to help the nurses care for the sick child. In schools too, open days are more common than they once were, but much hard thinking needs to be done if we are to discover the real importance and essential character of parent-teacher co-operation.

The teacher, as we have just said, is obliged to make an act of faith in the general effect of the school as a community upon the new little pupil. It is difficult for an adult, even for the teacher, to put himself in the child's place and appreciate the nature and extent of the shock which he experiences when he finds he is one of a large crowd of unknown companions. For most of the day he is kept in a room with a smaller number of companions but at times he is sent out into a large yard to face two or three hundred more. The whole appearance of the world of persons has changed, and father and mother are not there to give him a sense of security. The reaction of the new boy will vary according to whether he is alone or among friends in the crowd. If he has an elder brother or sister who can initiate him into his new status, he will learn one of the most essential facts of life. He will discover that the true gateway to a useful public life is through the sympathy and help of other people. If he has to struggle unaided, he may succeed in finding his niche, but often at a price. His aggressive tendencies may be over-exercised and so introduce into his relationships an element of truculence which will make him feared but not loved. The dangers of this precarious eminence for his future status in society are obvious.

On the other hand, an isolated child may sink into a quasi-anonymity by retiring into himself and by leading a kind of schizophrenic existence, remaining a centre of interest at home and living in a world of his own imagining at school. Such a double life will obviously affect the development of the pattern of his relationships and the growth of his sexuality. There are as many different possibilities as there are children. Each home, each school, as well as each child, is unique. The younger child in a large family experiences his school life differently from the only child. Physical health and stamina also have a bearing, and parents are only too familiar with the influence other children have upon their own. Manners, speech and behaviour undergo a transformation at school. The teacher's influence here is far less than is generally supposed. Classroom discipline may be excellent, but the standards of speech and conduct outside it are largely determined by the pupils themselves.

The child is taught to read and write. Enough has been written to convince us that the problem of literacy is not the problem of acquiring and using a technique. What matters is not that men and women should be able to read but that they should be able to tell a good piece of writing from a bad one. Writing is a means of communication and evil communication of any kind corrupts good manners. We are concerned here, however, with the initiation of the child into the two skills which are judged essential to education in our time. When he is learning to read his letters and write with his pen, he is entering a world of conventional symbols. Hitherto he has expressed himself in the words of his mother tongue and his communication has been limited to and by the spoken language and his own imagination. Now he is made free of a means of communication which will enlarge his sphere of relationship and influence to an almost unlimited extent.

He is not aware of this. He is struggling to transfer the symbols into sounds and the sounds into symbols—symbols which are not of his own invention. There are momentous options lurking in the spelling and copy books. They open the way to communication with the great minds of past, present and future. At the same time they present dangers. In our objective, Western culture, these are of two kinds. The most obvious risk lies in the enormous mass of trivial, paltry, vicious reading matter which fills the bookstalls and threatens to debase the currency of written communication. Far less evident is the obsession of objectivity which is the neurosis of Western culture today. The technique of reading admits the child to the whole range of writing in his own language. He will find abundant matter to attract and influence him. But the school curriculum will concentrate his attention chiefly on books which call for the exercise of his thought function. Admittedly, there will be scope too, especially in the literature lessons, for the development of his feeling function. The sensation and the intuition functions will, however, be more or less neglected. And there is the further complication of the introverted and extroverted attitudes. An extrovert child with a highly charged sensation function at school will be forced to treat in an introverted manner any stimuli to its exercise which he may find in his reading. His natural outward looking movement will be reversed. This may have serious consequences. He may find he does not make progress and a feeling of inferiority may ensue. If the teacher, seeking the cause of this backwardness, attributes it uncritically to idleness and tries to persuade the parents to support the application of those remedial measures deemed necessary, the pattern of the child's family relationships may be disturbed and deep wounds inflicted on the growing psyche.

These truths may be unwelcome to teachers and parents alike. They will object that if these complicated issues bedevil such tasks as teaching the child to read and write, then parent-hood and the teaching profession are beyond the powers of any ordinary human being. The child had better be handed over to a team of psychologists and escape the risk of permanent maim-ing. It is not my intention to reduce readers to such desperate straits, but I must point out the very real problems that exist. In a very large number of cases the origin of sexual maladjust-ment, misconduct, misery and ill-health is to be found in the false relationships which have been allowed to prevent many of our contemporaries from reaching adult status. To think that we can prevent these by a few lessons in sexual biology is surely singularly naïve. It is far better that we should be aware of the immense possibilities for good and evil that are present in early years. Nature, it must be emphasized, works towards the integration of the personality. If we are conscious of the options inherent in such situations as those of school life, we are already on the side of nature. It is the adoption of easy answers to the child's difficulties which is so dangerous. When, in a fit of bad temper, we accuse a child thoughtlessly of idleness, without having tried to find out whether there are other causes for his backwardness, it is we who are lazy and our accusation is a projection on to him of our own uncon-scious idleness.

An exaggerated emphasis on book culture and literary ex-pression tends to make us impatient with those whose psychological make-up hinders them from using reading and writing as their main vehicles of communication. Most teachers are aware of the variations which exist in their pupils in this respect. They realize the need for making allowances for them, but they are baulked in their efforts to do so by the class situa-tion, which is modelled upon the lecture room of the university. They are frustrated, too, by the requirements of a syllabus which is largely determined by the pressure of a highly in-dustrialized and politically conscious community. Teacher and pupil are in an equivocal position. Is the school to be the organ of the handing on of national and racial traditions from generation to generation? If so, the psychological peculiarities of the individual child are of primary importance if the teacher is to acquire a technique flexible enough to cope with the situation. Or is the school to be used principally to prepare the pupil for adaptation to life in the contemporary world? If so, the balance of the curriculum and the style of teaching will demand a conditioning of teacher and child to a given pattern of contemporary realities, a pattern which moreover is constantly changing.

The role of the parents in all this may not seem obvious, yet it is primordial. If the child is kept within the embrace of their mutual love the problems of the school are capable of solution. If the child is encouraged to grow and communicate freely with his father and mother without pampering or inhibiting, if they are conscious of him as a person in his own right, then he will have no fear of revealing in his own way the difficulties that he is facing. The immense resources of the family will be there to counteract the inevitable weaknesses of the school. There is no need for the parents to be learned or even aware of the findings of the psychologists. The love of man and wife as it envelops the child is a force which of itself works towards the perfection of the personalities involved in it. Still less should parents fear the influence of the school or debate as to whether they should keep the child at home and educate him there entirely. Although some people are able to satisfy the authorities that they can provide suitable instruction for their children at home, it is doubtful whether it is wise for them to take advantage of the fact. In modern society the school is essential for the child since it gives him the best opportunity of initiation into the life of the community. If he is deprived of this experience he may develop eccentricities which are signs of self-assertion rather than of integration.

Only brief allusion can be made to the very real problems

class distinction raises in the school. Even at an early age these may be a source of bewilderment and suffering to a sensitive child. They are relevant to the main thesis of this essay, since the class question is of importance in the choice of a partner for life. The English custom of segregating the young into schools on a class basis may not be quite so unjust and inhuman as it often seems. There are still something more than vestigial elements of a class society in this country and the segregation of children has this to be said for it—that it reduces the tension that a child has to endure at this critical stage. Tension is not a bad thing. It is both inevitable and necessary. But the child has enough of it when he meets the outside world in the school. He should not have to bear the additional weight of the class system. If that system is to be modified or abolished, it is surely too much to ask the children of the nation to undertake the task. The question of social structures and their relations to a class culture is a burning one which should occupy the minds of mature men and women. It is a problem of *adult* education.

No book on the general theme of sex can pass over the problem which the majority of parents find the most formidable of all, that is, the sex instruction of their children. It is during the school years that they are most conscious of the difficulties this raises. Although much that is said and written upon the subject seems to me superficial and even dangerous, I can only suggest here some lines of thought which may help to clarify the problem if not to solve it. I do not deny that parents are under a grave moral obligation to see that this instruction is given. They alone are in a position to know the needs of their own children and so are ideally the best persons to instruct them. Unfortunately, they are often so unintegrated themselves, so bound to surviving adolescent attitudes that, in practice, they are often more or less incapable of providing the essential background of unselfish love for one another and their offspring without which any mere explanation of the biological and anatomical facts is likely to do more harm than good.

Yet, on the face of it, it seems odd that the problem should ever arise. After all, other animal species copulate instinctively while the human young presumably have to be told how and why coitus is achieved. Our primary consciousness makes us aware of sexual passion, but it does not seem to do much more than this, although it may make us realize that we need guidance and instruction. Observation of primitive peoples suggests that in some societies children are left to experiment and to discover for themselves how their sexual organs work, while with others there is a ritual of initiation. In any case, the human situation is very different from that of the rest of the animals, whose instinct seems to suffice. With us the relation of sexuality to generation and the phenomena of consciousness seems to deliver us from the rule of the instinct and to place our whole sexual life under the law of relation. In a community such as our own, it would be the height of folly to pretend that nature, although its main urge is towards integration, would without conscious direction lead our children to a healthy sexual development.

When the child leaves home for the school—even if only for a few hours a day—the parent becomes anxious on the score of sexual instruction. But what of the child? Is it at this stage that it too becomes aware of strange, new movements within its own body and mind and seeks to learn their meaning? There is no adequate answer to this question. We need statistical evidence which is hard to come by and whose reliability would be doubtful. We should require the witness of large numbers of people able and willing to tell us how they came to know the laws of generation and the mechanism of sex. It is probable that, in a great number of cases, we should find that the desire to know the mystery of one's own origin comes before the actual interest in the sex organ. The child is used to the evacuatory functions of these and, unless he is given

precise information, will not have any idea that they are related to generation. In the case of the boy, erection will eventually occur at the onset of puberty, and he will be puzzled or
frightened without necessarily realizing—unless he has been
told—that it has anything to do with sexual activity. It will
often be the case that he has learned of the generative use of
the sex organs from other boys before he has experienced any
sex urges himself.

The anxiety that the parents feel has very deep roots, of
which they may not be conscious. It is not merely that they
sense the need to give the child the instruction which must
come sooner or later; it is not even, at this stage, a fear of the
child being perverted. It is rather that the parents realize, however vaguely, the whole social implications of the child's sexuality. The child has been incorporated into a social group
larger than the family. His sexual powers will be influenced
by the new environment, directly or indirectly, because he is
among children who are not in the same relation to him as his
brothers and sisters. The school is the first major step towards
adult sexuality and marriage, since the child already meets in
it those "others" from whom eventually he will choose his
life's partner.

At the heart of the parents' anxiety lies this sense of the
critical situation in which the child finds itself in regard to its
sexuality, as well and as much as in regard to the other physical and mental powers which now begin to develop in a new
and even frightening way. The question to be answered is twofold. What shall the child be told? Who shall tell him? Ideally
the parents should initiate him into the mysteries of sexuality.
Breezy amateur sexologists have no doubts on this point. They
do not hesitate to urge parents to instruct their children. Such
advice is easier to give than to take. All other forms of instruction, even in moral matters, are relatively simple to
provide, since they do not directly involve the relationship
between child and parent. I can tell my boy not to steal and

give him reasons why he should not do so. I can teach him to be truthful or to obey lawful authority. But when I begin to talk to him about sex, I feel embarrassed. Am I the victim of some religious or social taboo? I think not. There is much more than prudery at the root of my discomforture. I am, in fact, stripping myself before the child, revealing to him the source of his own being in his mother's and my own sexuality. It may be difficult to see why this is a painful process, but it is.

Much of the embarrassment arises from the confusion implied in the first question. With the question of what the child shall be told we become immediately aware of the biological and anatomical facts. This is to take an objective view, like those who think farmers' children are easier to instruct because they are used to the sexual behaviour of animals, or like those who imagine human sexuality can be best explained in the biology laboratory of the school. This is crudely to objectivize a profoundly subjective and personal reality. The physical facts have to be told to the child; but to give them priority is another matter. In the family circle, a start is often made when a baby is about to be born. The other children can be told that it is alive in their mother's womb. Yet this does not solve the main problem of instruction about the facts of intercourse. Perhaps these facts are not so important to the young child as the adult might think. We often assume that children are as deeply immersed as their elders in the Western habit of reducing reality to a series of objects. The child is frequently more of a philosopher in this respect than his parents. The great legends of the race, which are the vehicle of profound psychological wisdom, are a delight to him. His consciousness is far more open to the themes of the unconscious than that of adults. He will not find it hard to grasp the main principle of life producing life if it is told to him not merely or even primarily as a scientific truth, but by way of the symbol.

The answer to the question, What shall he be told? is therefore in one sense easy. He should be told what his parents know he can take and in a manner suited to his age and temperament. Children vary enormously in this as in other respects. No cast-iron rule can be laid down. Some children are known to begin masturbation habits as a result of sex instruction; others fall into these ways for lack of it. It is not so much the information that matters as the person who gives it and the one who receives it. Some fathers are the last persons to be entrusted with this delicate task. There are boys who have learned something of sexual relations from other lads for whom they have a real and healthy regard and, although the information has been given in a crude and joking fashion, little harm has resulted in the long run.

If the relations between parents and children are what they ought ideally to be, the normal child will as often as not put questions to father or mother at the time when he begins to be puzzled about his own origins. When this is the case, the parent has far less difficulty in explaining in general and particular terms what sexuality is and does. Unfortunately, such easy relations are by no means the rule and the second question—who shall tell him?—receives all sorts of strange answers. If the whole meaning of sexuality is to be conveyed, and in a way the child can understand, the moment at which instruction is given is of prime importance. I am assuming that the reader will agree that to explain the biology of generation without dealing with the ultimate human purpose of sex is little short of criminal. Who then is suited, if the parents are not, to decide when and how information is to be given and to undertake the task himself?

Frankly I do not know, though I believe that the problem, which is one of immense social significance, should not be thought out merely at the level of the individual child and family. There is need for a new sexual "climate". The customs of certain primitive peoples have something to teach us here. The initiation of the young into adult life is not confined to a narrow biological instruction; the passage from childhood to manhood is marked by an elaborate ceremonial in which symbolism, ascetic exercises and religious rites all combine to make this promotion a solemn engagement by which the young man enters into the heritage of tribal tradition, duty and privilege. It would be ridiculous to suggest a slavish copying of such practices. Yet the principles lying behind them, the sense of the community's responsibility, are well worth our attention and demand to be translated into a far more vigorous public conscience about sexual matters. The present sexual climate in England, resulting as it does from the timorous prudery of a previous age and the irresponsible adolescent reaction to it, is a major obstacle to the healthy development of our children. They have to live in a world where adolescent and immature attitudes to sex are rampant in press, cinema, radio, literature. The parents' work is often ruined by the crass puerility of so-called adults in this matter of life and death to a whole race.

It is a fact, incredible though it may seem, that the most "advanced" young people can come to marriage, after numerous sexual adventures on the way, with the most inadequate knowledge of the realities of the sex relation even at the physical level. Pathological distortions of the generative functions, and of the mental and spiritual aspects of sex, are frequently considered of more importance than the full, sound knowledge of integrated sexuality which alone can assure the complete union of man and woman as persons and provide for their children that community of spiritual and physical love which they need if they are to grow into fully human manhood and womanhood. It is a dangerous state of affairs when our young people know all the tricks of contraception but have only the vaguest notion of how the marriage act is to be performed if it is to give the maximum physical and psychological satisfaction to the woman; when they learn what love and marriage are from films, the press, the glossy magazines and popular songs.

Of all the social forces that affect personal development the school is probably the most powerful at the pre-puberty stage, but something must also be said here of other influences which play their part. They need far more detailed study than I can give them, yet a brief outline of some of the ways in which they too contribute to the growth of personality, and therefore to the adult attitude to sex, may suggest lines of thought and observation which the reader will wish to follow up on his own account.

The child enters the houses of other people who may be friends of his parents or the families of boys he meets at school. This admission to what is to him another world has curious and important effects upon his awareness. We are all familiar with his claim that the jam and cakes from next door taste far better than his mother's, that his friend's father is a far more humane and understanding man than his own. A little later, the boy will find that his friends' sisters are infinitely more mysterious and fascinating than his own. This enlarging of consciousness introduces him to the mystery of the "other" in a way that his own family cannot yet do, for it is still the womb from which he has to emerge psychologically if he is to become an independent person in his own right. There is an atmosphere of liberty and spontaneity in the neighbour's house which he cannot find in his parents'. Although he may not be aware of it, he now begins to penetrate the veils which hide the mystery of the love of husband and wife.

In his own home the relations of father and mother are too bound up with his own involvement in their life for him to be able to see them as lovers. If he is included, as he should be, in their love, he will live by and in it to such an extent that he cannot observe and know it as a fact separate from his own existence. If they quarrel he will be too insecure to puzzle his brain over their relationship. It will be a source of anguish and unspoken fear. But in the neighbour's house he is a spectator, he can look with a clear vision at the pattern of relationships which hold the family together. The affection of the parents for one another, the intimacy of father, mother and children are a revelation to him. He becomes acutely conscious of himself as an outsider, as a person who enters into voluntary relations with others. No wonder that he finds life in their company a much more exciting affair than his existence at home.

This new type of relationship soon leads however to the time when he too invites his friends to his home. He then sees that for them, his own family is just as wonderful a society as theirs for him. All this is a vital experience for boys and girls and essential both to their ultimate conscious understanding of their own family and to their own growth from childhood to adult status. As regards sexuality, the "other" family—unaware of the fact though the child is—introduces him to a group whose very existence is the result of generation and sexual activity in which he himself is not involved. He is meeting sexuality as an objective fact. He may have seen his own parents embracing and kissing one another and have felt acutely embarrassed. Here is something mysterious in which he is in some way included yet excluded at one and the same time. His growing sense of his own objective existence makes him both puzzled and in some degree jealous when he sees signs and tokens of affection exchanged between father and mother. But if he witnesses similar love-making in another family, his reaction is different. He is curious and excited, even if he has as yet no knowledge of the facts of sex.

Both his school life and his experience of families other than his own and the normal process of development, lead him to the stage at which he begins to take an interest in girls of his own age. The phenomenon of calf-love needs investigation. It is usually innocent enough where the family background is sound, but in other cases it may mark the beginning of premature sexual activity. Many children, however, start little love affairs before they have been told the anatomical facts of sex. Even where there is a less innocent relationship, it is obviously not based on love in the true sense of the word. The child is developing in the second degree of relation and children of the opposite sex are little more than objects which excite his curiosity and give him opportunities to assert himself. This he may do by entering into rivalry with other boys and so throw himself into a struggle with them for the "affections" of some small girl. In boarding schools, where children are segregated from the other sex, this groping for an objective relationship with others will often take a homosexual form and small boys run the risk of developing feminine attitudes to the older ones. This is a problem that requires thorough and honest examination. It is not attempted here, since only a minority of the nation's boys and girls are sent to boarding schools. We would only insist that the new degree of relation which they attain between the ages of five and eleven demands that those in charge of them should be aware that the change of attitude towards others which is its chief characteristic cannot fail to have important repercussions in the sexual sphere. Children are bound to reach this stage and it is the duty of the adult to see that they are discreetly guided through it in all branches of their activity in such a way that they emerge from it to the third degree of relation instead of remaining fixed in an attitude of self-centred objectivity.

Large numbers of children never go to a place of worship. I am not concerned with the effect of this upon their religious sense. I am only considering church and chapel as communities influencing the child in its personal development. Those who never have contact with them are deprived of important psychological aids to growth. Those who are regular attendants at their services and meetings profit from these, but are also exposed to certain real dangers. Every human society is a battleground of good and evil and the religious community in so far as it is a human institution is not exempt from this law. Some religious bodies are more or less committed to an attitude towards sex which makes it a rule that it should never be mentioned in the pulpit, the Sunday school or the Bible class. To throw young people together without some clear teaching on sexuality and marriage and an honest approach to the difficulties that we meet in our sexual life is to ask for trouble. There is an unhealthy atmosphere of romantic love on the one hand and of a secretive, unconfessed obsession with the genital facts which does harm among many religious groups.

It is fatally easy, too, for a growing child to acquire the notion that religion deals with celestial things and that his body is something with its own laws. The dichotomy of body and mind which we mentioned in the first chapter can become firmly fixed in him and poison his whole life. He has what we might almost call a schizophrenic attitude to sex. It appears to him as a necessary evil from which religion temporarily delivers us while we are exalted above ourselves in the splendour and warmth of community worship. When the cosy protective atmosphere of the Sunday evening service gives way to the bleak rays of Monday morning's sun, we return to the world, that pool of iniquity in which we have to struggle for our daily bread. But to him the "world" of the New Testament is not the good earth which God created—and man and woman created he them in his own image—it is the world of the objective self, the world of self-seeking in which others are the instruments of our advancement or our pleasure. Many religious bodies do not make this distinction clear and the child grows up with terrible fears and inhibitions which may ultimately drive him in despair away from all doctrine and worship into a life of instinct uncontrolled by the great and noble cosmic purposes of sexuality, marriage and love.

Where the sacrament of penance is practised and the child is taught from an early age to examine his conscience and to confess his sins, there is less danger of such distortion. Yet here much will depend on the priest who hears the confession and on those who prepare the child to make it. If it is made clear to him in a way that he can understand that sex is good but that it may be diverted from its purpose by self-love and the lust which is self-love's most obvious manifestation, he will learn to dissociate the evils which self-seeking produces from erroneous notions about the nature of sex itself. He will be spared the agony of scruples and the stunting influence of inhibitions.

The life of a religious society offers a fruitful training in true altruism. The child is brought into touch with a historical community having long traditions, and is made far more conscious of this than in the school, where lessons and personal relationships occupy the forefront of his awareness. Where there is a strong sense of historical continuity, the child is made conscious both of his inclusion in this greater community spanning time and space and also of his place and duty. It is, in short, a royal road to the third degree of relation. He will be present at baptisms, weddings and funerals and so will be brought into contact with the fundamental realities of human life in a community setting. The value of this experience may not always be appreciated. I believe that it is very great indeed. At these crucial moments in the life of the family, the community and the individual, we are all of us, if only for a short period, made aware of the depths of meaning which lie within us below the superficialities which we so often call by the noble name of "life". The great questions concerning human destiny beat upon the mind with an inexorable force at such times and even the child in his simple way is not unaware of them. Later in life it will be within the context and stream of a historic community, both civil and religious, that he will have to work out the implications of his own sexuality. It is well for him to experience this inclusion in a living society in a form where it is clearly obvious to him. From this point of view the religious bodies are irreplaceable.

We may well wonder what will be the ultimate effect upon

us of a wholly secularized life. This is a new thing. The pre-Christian pagan societies were profoundly religious. The modern West is moving towards a form of individual and social existence in which there will be no room for, no consciousness of, ultimate values. What kind of sexual practice is such a state of mind likely to produce? Apart from all considerations as to the truth of religious doctrines, it is obvious, as the psychologists have shown, that primordial religious themes work in our unconscious minds and if they are not given some external expression they will be projected unconsciously on to institutions and persons. The worship of status, of sex, of the film star and the popular singer are surely examples of this distortion of the religious sense. The absolute value given by many today to their genital passions appears to be an instance of the deification of the world of creatures, the modern form of the worship of Venus. And it is the deadlier because it is an unconscious form of religion.

The whole pattern of the child's relations with others is modified as he grows. Another phenomenon of growth is the "gang". In his middle childhood, the boy tends to join small groups of lads like himself, and to play all kinds of wild and vigorous games with them. This rough and ready organization, for which the children are wholly responsible, is important for their development. It seems that they realize they are not yet fit for an independent personal existence, but find the family insufficient for their needs. The "gang" is an intermediate group between the womblike family and the vast organism of society. In a sense children are aware of the gigantic community which is to be the environment of their adult life and they league themselves against it. They feel they must join together to defend themselves from its huge anonymous forces. Each child is too small to play David alone against this Goliath. Together they can cope with it and assure their independence against family and State at least as a group. Is the present problem of "gangs" of young men who might be expected to have outgrown this mentality partly due, perhaps, to a regression on the part of their members to this early stage? Their sexual promiscuousness appears to be an adult version of the "games" the children's gang plays with such excitement and enjoyment.

Sex is absent from the children's gang. The aim of most of their group games seems to be precisely that objective self-assertion which is characteristic of the second degree of relation. Each lad tries to be "the king of the castle". It almost seems that any reference to the opposite sex is taboo. When the boys want to talk about their growing curiosity in sexual matters they do so in pairs or in very small groups. Many learning in this way the anatomical facts in a crude and incomplete manner. There is often one "hero" who is supposed to have had intercourse and is considered to be a real man in consequence. Smutty stories begin to be exchanged in these inner circles and as the lads come nearer to their puberty, the "gang" is deserted first in favour of these coteries; later, in the full *sturm und drang* of adolescence, a period of isolation sets in, during which the only survival of the earlier community mentality is the friendships which have been formed with one or two other boys. And these often endure in later life.

Movements such as the Scouts seek to harness the natural phases of development to an ideal—service of others, healthy mental and physical development, acquisition of skills, a true and lasting sense of duty to the community at large. All such training I believe to be of value in the general growth from childhood to manhood. Is there any directly sexual development which they foster? It is difficult to say. The Scout Law insists that a Scout should be pure in thought, word and deed, but what does this promise mean to the boy? All will depend on what he knows of sex as cosmic force. The dangers inherent in any merely anatomical account of sex mechanisms and the threat of radical misunderstanding due to a false notion of purity have already been mentioned. Any teaching which suggests that sex in itself is just an animal function will make it all but impossible for the boy to acquire in due course a genuine human and adult attitude towards women. Most scoutmasters avoid mentioning sexual matters to their troops and this is perhaps just as well. The movement seeks to canalize the "gang" and the small group mentalities into useful and healthy activity and in so far as it succeeds in doing this, it will have provided a good background to developing sexuality.

One danger, however, should be taken into account. If it is essential that young people should not look upon sex as a regrettable animal survival in the human race, it is equally important that they should not adopt what we may call a romantic view of the opposite sex. I shall have more to say on this in a later chapter. At the present point in the argument, I would only suggest that many of the sexual difficulties met with in the next phase, that is in adolescence, arise from a double standard of values. A boy will develop an unreal, romantic and almost idolatrous affection for a girl, while at the same time indulging either in masturbation or superficial sexual activities with other young women. He learns to separate the ideal of love from sexuality, and that is a thoroughly bad preparation for marriage. The notion of knighthood which forms part of the ethos of many youth movements has to be carefully purged of this false romanticism. Much harm can be done by telling a boy that he has to treat other girls as though they were his sisters. This is to ask the impossible. No good is ever done by refusing to face facts. Purity must be presented as a positive virtue, not as a mere abstention from immoral acts.

It is often said that modern mass media of entertainment— cinema, radio, television—have a harmful effect on the young. There seems sufficient evidence to prove that, until children reach puberty, the sexual immaturity of many films, plays and variety shows has hardly any influence. The dangers are of another kind. It has been argued that television, for instance (and the same applies to radio), is an invasion of the home.

People of all kinds are admitted, often enough quite indiscriminately, and allowed to communicate with the children of the family through a medium which, especially in the case of television, has a very powerful impact on the imagination. The danger here lies not so much in the things these distant visitors say and do, as in the fact that they are in a position of such power.

In normal family relations, there is a two-way communication. Whatever we say or do in the family circle will be commented on. We are questioned about our opinions. We have to answer for our conduct. The children may be warned not to make frank comments about visitors at least while they are in the house; they cannot be stopped from doing so when the family is alone again. But those who enter our homes on wireless and television sets are in a privileged position. They call the tune. The family is a mere bundle of spectators. There is no give and take and so this exalted situation of the speaker, the actor or the singer introduces a new dimension of relationship. The child, precisely at the stage when it is struggling to disentangle its own personality from the womb of the family, is sucked down into another womblike experience. Its eyes are fixed on the screen. It is in a state of semi-hypnosis, in a world of dreams.

Not that this is a bad thing. On the contrary, the mass media of entertainment like every other human device have their opportunities for doing both good and evil. It is essential to realize what is happening when a child, or for that matter a grown-up, is subjected to their powerful influence. Only then can we hope to avoid the evil and promote the good effects. The world of dreams is a human one and rightly interpreted and integrated into our waking life is of enormous value. The interpretation and the integration are everything. We are not sufficiently familiar yet with the long-term effects of mass entertainment to judge how far its potentialities for good are, or even can be, realized. At present, all we can do is to make sure that they are not allowed to become a narcotic substitute for living.

As I have already pointed out, the school has a profound influence on the development of personality and hence on its sexual evolution. The experiment of secondary education for all introduces a new element and a new problem into the life of most English children. It is too early yet to assess the effects of the separation of the eleven-plus pupils into the three types of secondary school. Certain results are apparent and give rise to much comment and suggestions for reform; the proposed general establishment of comprehensive schools is an instance. But there is one fact which is not discussed although it is surely of the highest importance: the child has to face both its puberty crisis and adaption to a new form of education at the same period of its life. This has always been the case with children going from the primary to the grammar school, but it has now become a problem facing every child.

As things now stand, when a pupil reaches the age of eleven the educational authorities decide whether he is suited for grammar, secondary or technical education and, rightly or wrongly, this decision is considered by parents and children as a judgment on their intellectual powers; the drafting of a boy or girl to a secondary school is taken to mean that the child is inferior to those who are chosen for the grammar school. However regrettable and irrational this is, it is a common reaction and a formidable weakness which educationalists have to recognize.

Our only concern with this matter in the context of this book is to take note of the inevitable effects upon the child of a strong inferiority feeling at this critical stage of its general and sexual development. It is common knowledge that such feelings lead to compensatory behaviour. We are all of us liable to adopt lines of conduct and thought which will bolster up our sense of personal value when we find that value called in question or denied, and it is surely not unlikely that the awakening genital urge in the puberty phase will cause the child to develop a pre-cocious and self-centred interest in sexual activity. In the case of the grammar school pupil, the educational authorities have passed what is still considered to be a favourable judgment on the child's powers. In a large number of cases, their assessment of the intelligence and suitability of the boy or girl for a more academic type of education will prove valid in the event. Nobody will claim that the grammar school population lives in perfect sexual innocence, but it is true that the general style of life and learning in the grammar school encourages interests which will, to say the least, distract the pupil from an excessive preoccupation with his sexual development. It is true also that an over-emphasis on intellectual growth raises its own partic-ular problems in the sexual field. Recent research has shown that, among adults, sexual maladjustment is common among men belonging to the intellectual strata of our society.

There seems to be some evidence to suggest that a certain proportion of children in modern secondary schools seek com-pensation for their supposed intellectual inferiority in the sexual sphere. There is no reason for us to be surprised or shocked at this. Rather should the realities of the child's situa-tion stir us to do some hard thinking about the whole question of what the secondary modern school is and what it ought to attempt to do. The puberty crisis is one of the most trying through which children pass. To pretend that the school can ignore it and take no account of it in working out the mode of life and study the children are to adopt is little short of criminal.

The basic distinction between the secondary modern school and the grammar school lies presumably in the field of function. Psychology has made it clear that such functions as thought, sensation, feeling and intuition, although present in us all, do not reach the same level of consciousness in every person. We are primarily men of thought, or of sensation, or of feeling or of intuition. The grammar school pupil is presumed to have shown that he will develop chiefly through the exercise and development of his thought function. The secondary modern child is supposed to show possibilities of growth in the sphere of one of the other three functions. As sensation is likely to be the commonest of these, it is inevitable that sexual development should lead to direct interest in its physical manifestations. This possibility must be faced.

For the more intellectual child, the problem is different; there is a danger here of a dual mentality. Academic studies with their strong abstract character may occupy one part of the personality while sexual urges may become a real and terrifying obsession, giving rise to a more introverted activity than is the case with the child who lives largely by sensation. The latter has not to exist in so rarefied an intellectual atmosphere and lives, if I may so put it, more in his body. Educationalists have seen the danger and most grammar schools have increasingly improved their standard of physical education and their playing field facilities. This is all to the good, although it cannot be considered as a total solution to the problem.

There is another aspect of grammar school education which is relevant to the main argument of this book. The old idea of learning for learning's sake has largely disappeared and the pupil nowadays tends to look upon knowledge as a means to an end, and the end in most cases is a good job in later life. In this attitude he is aided and abetted often by his parents, sometimes even by the teacher, especially where examination results are held to be the chief criterion of the school's achievement. Where knowledge and learning are treated in this way they soon cease to have any reality of their own. They become a mass of information to be digested and memorized for the sake of a certificate, or even a scholarship to the university. The effect of this etiolated, false intellectual activity upon the sexual development of the child requires consideration and investigation. Where knowledge is real and vital and impinges on experience at every turn then there is far more hope that the great upsurges of sexual passion may be seen as part of the whole business of living. Where knowledge appears as a mere abstraction or as a means to an end, then the contrast between the vital sexual forces and the dessicated mind is acute and may easily lead to the near schizophrenic attitude previously discussed.

It is obvious therefore that the whole question of the influence of the school on the growth of the personality and the development of sexuality demands far more attention than it now receives from teachers, educationalists and parents. The sexual factor in the child's school life is generally brushed aside in educational theory and practice, as a private affair between parents and child. There is a sense in which this is right and proper. I am not advocating mass sexual instruction in schools. I do suggest that the whole life of the school, the planning of its curriculum, the relations of parent and teacher are vital matters which, far from being mere administrative problems, are of the utmost importance to the personal and sexual development of the child.

III

The Crisis of Adolescence

THE SEXUALITY of the adolescent is two-headed, Janus-like. He becomes aware of his own body as an object able to give him a pleasure far more intense and ultimately of a different kind than any he has hitherto experienced. At the same time he is attracted towards other persons of his own or the other sex. It is not uncommon for this attraction, although springing from the nascent genital urge, to be free from sexual curiosity and from any direct desire for physical experience. Timidity, inhibitions, fear of consequences—all these may prevent him from entering into a full or partial sexual relation with others. There may also be a genuine beginning of love which in some obscure way keeps him from tampering with the body of the person who awakens this feeling. He will, however, be fortunate if he avoids the use of his own sexual organs for the sole purpose of pleasure. The fact of masturbation is serious and important enough for its implications in the general development of the personality to be examined; but for the moment, however, it is merely to be noted that it shows clearly that the boy has now reached the stage when even his own body is objectivized and present to him as a means of pleasure.

This genital pleasure is different in kind from all others. This is because it has a double effect. During the preliminaries to orgasm the body, whether one's own or another's, is an object which we are tempted to use solely for our own ends. At the climax of the act, there is an ecstasy of feeling which enlarges the sense of one's own subjective being and in true hetero-sexual union, the sense, too, of that of the partner's being. It is at this point that the pleasure is unique for reasons which will be examined in a later chapter. Meanwhile, something must be said, however briefly, of the nature of pleasure in general, for sexual joy has its roots in the quest for pleasure which is a mark of human activity.

Pleasure is an experience of the primary consciousness and therefore difficult to describe. The data of the primary consciousness cannot be objectivized without being deformed. They are immediate experiences and to translate them into terms of the secondary consciousness is to take them from their own realm of reality and so radically to alter our view of them. The aesthetic experience of a man listening to music cannot be described solely in terms of the physics of sound. Nor can a satisfactory explanation be given by analysing the form, sequence and pattern of the work which he is hearing. Such objective treatment has value in its own order. It may even provide pointers to the *raison d'être* of the aesthetic experience itself. But it cannot describe that experience. Experiences of the primary consciousness cannot truly be described, they can only be *named*. When we name them, others who have had similar experiences know exactly what we are talking about. The name itself is the term of a long and intricate process of social evolution inherited by each of us as our own personality develops in the context of our lives.

The meaning of pleasure is no more and no less than what the word signifies to those who have experienced the thing. The word is an audible symbol or sign and as such has *resonance* rather than meaning. A verbal definition of such words introduces a subtle but profound difference into our relation to the experience that we are trying to define. Newman's *cor ad cor loquitor* and Pascal's *raisons du coeur* are relevant here.

The phenomena accompanying, causing, indicating pleasure can be described, analysed and scientifically investigated. What eludes us is the reality of the experience itself. This does not imply that there is no genuine knowledge of that experience. On the contrary. Yet such knowledge derives from a deepening of our apprehension of the experience itself and of all that it brings to our inner life and our relations with others. It is said that the Eastern ascetics meditate for years at a time on the sound made by one clap of the hands. The echoes, the resonance within the mind of such words as "pleasure" can also give us knowledge which only contemplation can achieve.

It seems clear that, when we experience pleasure, there is a real sense of liberation, of freedom. Our energies seem to be released and made available to our conscious mind. All or most pleasures may originate in a physical operation, yet the direction which different pleasurable experiences impose upon our consciousness reveals that the essence of human pleasure lies beyond the body. Certain pleasures—eating and drinking, for example—direct our attention to an inner sensation of well-being, which is far more than the mere satisfaction of appetite. We are made more aware of ourselves as enriched, freed from a necessity which our previous hunger indicated. There are other pleasures—the aesthetic, for instance—in which the physical element is clearly no more than the necessary instrument and in no sense the essence of the experience. Such pleasures lead directly to what the French call a *prise de conscience*, while the more physical types of pleasure involve also a *prise de possession*. In the case of human relationships the whole idea of personal enrichment by means of a possession of other things and persons leads to that totally objective attitude which was mentioned previously as fatal to the true growth of the personality.

The critical passage from the second to the third degree of relationship involves a sacrifice of self, a reverent acceptance of the "other" as a subject in its or his own right. There is a sense therefore in which we have to achieve a heightened self-consciousness by an initial act which produces a temporary loss or diminution of consciousness. We have to give ourselves, we have to save our lives by losing them. If we refuse this sacrifice, if we treat "the other" as an object only, we eventually dull our own self-consciousness. A complete objectivity would deprive us altogether of self-awareness. In Jungian terms the integration of the personality demands that the Ego should give place to the Self, and the Self is both the individual person and—paradoxical though it may seem—others with whom he has established a true inter-subjective relationship. We find ourselves in those others. The pleasure therefore which the adolescent experiences in the sexual activation of his own body presents him with a challenge of the utmost importance for his future development.

Masturbation may arise under very different circumstances in different individuals. It may result from information given by other persons, from sexual manipulation by or with others of the same or of the opposite sex, or from sexual fantasies in the imagination of the individual concerned. For our present purpose we can leave aside the causes of the habit. Here we are concerned with the pleasure that it offers. Once the potentialities latent in it are examined, we shall be able to see the changes it introduces into the relations of the adolescent with himself, with his body and with other people. Before the puberty stage, the child's pleasures have originated chiefly in persons and things external to himself. Now for the first time —apart from any infantile masturbation which will have been forgotten—he discovers a source of intense pleasure which he can activate at will and which is entirely situated in his own body. Nascent genital functions are his first introduction to the depths and resources of his own individuality. Solitary masturbation is therefore ambivalent. On the one hand it gives a sense of personal power and self-sufficiency, on the other, it isolates the child from other people. Apart from moral considerations, it has a positive and a negative effect. Like every kind of pleasure, it brings a feeling of release from a previous more limited, more dependent existence and so admits to a hitherto unknown realm of experience, a new dimension of self-awareness. Then, too, it gives rise to a sense of separateness, a heightened realization of one's own isolated objective being. This dual movement in the personality inevitably forces the adolescent to become introverted. He passes through a stage when he no longer finds he needs the gang or the company of others. He is involved in a project which drives him inwards to explore the hidden places of his own being.

In some primitive societies, though by no means in all, adolescent sexual promiscuity is allowed, presumably in order to prevent this adolescent introversion from distorting the development of the personality. This is one solution to a vital problem. At the opposite extreme, certain sections of Western society have practised severe repression. Of the two, the former solution has the advantage of driving the new forces at work in an outward direction and so preventing them from poisoning the inner life and imprisoning the personality in an unnatural fear of a great cosmic force and of the pleasure that accompanies its manifestations. Of recent years, repression has been replaced by an attitude of exaggerated tolerance towards the masturbation habit. It has been held that boys have to go through this phase, that there is nothing we can do about it, that they will grow out of it, and that it is better to take no notice and to hope for the best. This new approach neglects the great issues involved in the crisis of adolescence. The human personality cannot be divided into separate compartments each having its own programme. The events which affect one side of our nature and modify one aspect of our behaviour influence the whole of our developing personality for good or evil.

There is abundant evidence to show that the ego-centricity produced by the masturbation habit has serious consequences for the character as a whole. Maladjustment in the marriage act can frequently be traced to this fixation which persists long after the physical habit has ceased. We may continue, that is, to find our sexual organs remain objects over which we have to exercise a difficult control instead of the means by which our unselfish love is expressed in sexual relations with our wife. We then have the impossible task of attempting to master a cosmic force by sheer will-power, whereas the secret of success lies in a total outward movement of mind and body to the person loved. Intercourse, to be a genuine manifestation of love, must be dominated by a contemplative attitude of the whole personality, a patient attention to the needs of the partner. It is precisely this attitude which the ego-fixation resulting from a long masturbatory habit makes so difficult to acquire.

A new, realistic view of the problem is needed. We must see all that is involved in it. In the terms of the first chapter, the adolescent has reached the stage when he meets the challenge of subjectivity. He has, that is, to learn that others are beings with rights of their own, that he himself is a subject with rights of his own. The sexual urges which he experiences present this challenge to him in a particularly insistent form. Masturbation is surely far more than a defiance of instinct launched in the face of reason. This interpretation was obviously in the mind of the lecturer who once told a class of young people training to become teachers that they should tell their pupils that sex was a purely animal thing and had to be controlled because, unfortunately, it was not customary to marry in our society when the genital organs first became capable of performing their reproductive function. This advice implies that marriage solves the problem of sexual control. It does nothing of the sort, at least in the sense the lecturer had in mind. There is no guarantee whatsoever that marriage considered solely as a legal institution will automatically relieve the partners from sexual deviations. This is surely because human sexuality is not just an animal function but a symbol of relationships. If, in most human societies, the puberty period is not generally considered to be the right time for marriage, it is not merely that boys and girls are not sufficiently economically independent, but because the group realizes that their personal growth in relationships is not yet complete. Masturbation is the outward manifestation of the inward struggle to pass to the third degree of relationship at which the self is fully realized as a subject related to other subjects. There are many other signs of this inward struggle, some of which are briefly considered later in this chapter, but it is the sexual one which is the most obvious and the most powerful in its influence and effects.

The habit of masturbation is primarily a symbol of the temporary divorce between consciousness and bodily existence which has so often given rise to the doctrine of spirit versus flesh, reason and will versus instinct and passion. The adolescent experiences a new freedom, knows he is a subject and is tempted to treat his sexual organs as mere objects which give him pleasure. But consciousness will not let him rest in this dichotomy of soul and body. It is precisely at this period that he is attracted sexually to others. Here again a choice is implicit. His first genital movement is again objective, self-seeking. Sexuality is so urgent a force within him that his sense of his own increasing subjectivity and independence removes from the forefront of consciousness the fact that sexuality is the means of human reproduction. The purpose of this cosmic force is virtually divorced from its exercise.

The extreme form of this divorce is found in homosexual relations. Although this distressing state is receiving much attention at the moment, its etiology and symptomatology are far from being fully understood. Does hormonic development play a part? Probably not. Are psychological maladjustments the sole cause? It may well be so. Much more research is needed before we can say that we have solved the mystery. One point however is established. Many homosexuals are acutely conscious of being abnormal and suffer intense shame; they are condemned to a sterile sexuality, a mere pleasure mechanism. It is true, of course, that there may be a genuine relation of love between homosexuals without any sexual manifestations; and such a genuine relationship may also arise between those who have sexual intercourse, but in this case their sexuality is an improper symbol of that love since the primary purpose of sex is clearly only fully realized in married love issuing in the birth of children.

True homosexuality seems to be a form of personality disorder, and it is possible that for this reason our notion of the range and scope of free choice needs revaluation. How far does a disorder of this nature govern compulsory mechanisms which may thus become all but irresistible? Where does free will end, disordered state begin? It is easy to be dogmatic on this subject. We know that such states as true kleptomania exist, and we know, too, to use theological terms, that the results of the Fall are not confined to the realm of the will, that disorders of mind, of personality, are as much our inheritance as disease of the body. There are cases where such disorders are no more the result of conscious choice of evil than are physical syndromes. Homosexuality may be, even if not always, a disorder of relationship making the complete passage to the third degree of intersubjective relation all but impossible.

Sexuality is only mature, adult, fully human, when it becomes the sign of the inner unity of the personality and of the union of the Self with other selves in utter reverence and total self-sacrifice. Freud may have sensed this when he taught that the death wish is the obverse of the sexual libido, though he does not seem to have investigated the profound meaning of the death wish itself. If we take it to be not merely a desire for rest, for entropy, but a longing to die to the ego so that we may be alive to the Self, we may indeed accept it as relevant to the growth of the personality.

During the first upsurge of sexual desire there is no true

focus for human sexuality. It is diffused and acts both as a blind physical impulse and as a source of fantasy. It is only when the whole force of its movement is finally directed towards one person that a higher and more specific level of primary consciousness is reached and the will to fatherhood begins to become self-evident. It is only when this entry into a higher sphere of consciousness is made that sexuality becomes capable of direction and so able to enrich the personality not only by its vital yet hitherto diffused power, but also by its assumption into the realm of the spirit. It is caught up in the greater mystery of love, the mystery of the union of I and Thou.

At the psychological level, the adolescent has to come to terms sooner or later with the Anima image. This, according to Jung, is the figure, the archetype of the feminine side of the male personality. Biologically, we are each of us a mixture of male and female. We experience the presence of the opposite sex in our own individuality in various ways. Psychologically, the image of the Woman, the mysterious, powerful creature of dreams and legends, is the bearer of the spheres of our own person of which we are not conscious. The sexual fantasies of youth are a mixture of biological urges and of this rising into consciousness of the hidden depths of the personality. It is only too easy for the adolescent to project the Anima image on to some real person. Hence the magical nature of first love. The loved one is not so much worshipped for herself as for the primeval myth she is made to carry—the Woman who can answer all our questions, reveal to us the mystery of ourselves. This first love may be, and often is, divorced from all genital passion, at least to begin with.

We saw above that adolescent sexual difficulties show clearly that it is possible to separate the sex impulse from its generative purpose. The primary physical urge in the male is to expel the spermatozoa. The pleasure the adolescent experiences is a result of self-abuse and sexual fantasy. Yet, at the same time, there is an absorbing interest in or affection for other persons, normally of the other sex. The fundamental direction of the instinct is obvious enough, the urge to union in the generative act. Yet the fact of masturbation creates a scandal, a contradiction in nature itself. How is it possible to divert a cosmic force from its proper channels and ends? How is it possible to use it as a means to pleasure apart from its generative purpose? The adolescent experience poses the immense mystery of freedom. It raises fundamental questions: Am I personally responsible for the activity of my body? How far can I and ought I to control it? Do I, and to what extent, transcend it? What is my relation to my body if I do transcend it? "I am my body," as Marcel says, "but I am not my life." Life I have received. It is greater than I. Perhaps I have obligations to it, since it is not mine. I may pretend that I am powerless in the grip of life, that I, like the rest of the animals, am merely a creature of instinct, a moment in the cosmic force. Yet self-consciousness is there to deny it, to reveal to me that, whether I like it or not, I move also in a realm where instinct cannot be absent or safely repressed, but can only be human in so far as it is assumed into that higher sphere of consciousness in which I live and move and have my being.

However pedestrian the existence of the majority of men, however immersed the life of the spirit may be in the material cares and joys of this world, there comes to each of us, if only during our puberty, this encounter with the very stuff of our spiritual nature, this mysterious meeting with the fact of freedom. And it is our sexuality above all which leads us into the presence of the mystery. We must face the facts of the relation of sex to liberty, of body to soul, of instinct to consciousness, of passion to act. All of these primordial realities are involved in the tragic options not only of the adolescent but of each of us in the evolution of our sexuality from childhood to old age. The urge to masturbation, we repeat, is more than a physical instinctive reaction to an interior or external stimulus. It is the instinctive drive which places us at the crossroads of our human existance and destiny and reveals in body and mind the ultimate realities by which we live. It raises the great questions—who am I? What ought I to do? in an acute peremptory form. It is the crisis of incarnation. Shall I, can I assume this movement into my self, into the person I am always becoming, and make it the outward expression of the spiritual reality which my consciousness tells me I am, since I *know* I exist?

Puberty and the urge to masturbation, then, bring the adolescent face to face with the mystery of freedom. In exceptional cases, the upsurge of sexual passion so dominates consciousness that the mere sight of a good-looking girl will produce ejaculation. Such cases are obviously pathological, but they are extreme forms of a general tendency during this period of life, the tendency, that is, to submit passively to the urges which sweep over soul and body. If freedom is sacrificed to instinct the way is open for a degeneration, a regression which, even if it does not lead to the mental condition called satyriasis, will reduce the adolescent and the man he is to become to a level lower even that that of the beasts. There is a state known to psychology as Donjuanism. It is due not to a heroic sexual generosity, as some would have us think, but to a virility which is defective owing to an auto-erotic attitude, which survives from the period of purely infantile relations with others. The personality is swallowed up in the sexual function and so loses its freedom.

To seek sexual pleasure solely for egoistic reasons is beyond the power of the other animals whose sexuality is controlled by the law of generation and its rhythms. It is sometimes argued—and the adolescent may be influenced by this piece of special pleading—that had man not evolved into a state of self-consciousness, his sexuality would have stayed under the absolute control of a cosmic law and an unerring instinct. The price of consciousness is therefore a conflict with an instinctual drive no longer under the rule of nature and all but impossible for man to master with his fragile reason and uncertain will. This suggestion implies that consciousness is contrary to nature, it is an accident, a sport. Yet, if the evolutionary doctrine is true, on what grounds do we deny that the emergence of human consciousness is an essential stage in the unfolding pattern of life?

The dichotomy solution to the practical difficulty may seem the best answer to an agonizing problem of conduct. Why not give full rein to instinct? Why not allow the body to be dominated by its sexual urges while we reserve our I-Thou relationships for purely spiritual intercourse? It may be that this idea was at the root of the Athenian cult of homosexuality. The man-wife relation was purely generative. The homosexual attachments, which, as Jowett noted, are the ancient equivalent of romantic love, began by being predominantly physical—a search for pleasure—and then led the soul from the realm of the senses to that of eternal truth and beauty. This teaching is found in Plato's Symposium. Admittedly it does not favour Donjuanism, yet it, too, by-passes the deep personal relations which should exist between husband and wife.

If this radical division of mind and body, instinct and freedom, is practised, we find ourselves in difficulties of every kind. Our state is one of conflict and mystery. There is no going back in one aspect of our life to the spontaneity of the beasts, while the mind soars into Olympus. The physical urges of man are those of a being who is as much soul as he is body. Sexuality in man has entered the realm of liberty, choice, reason, will, consciousness. It cannot return in him to the darkness of the unconscious. If we attempt to behave in what we call a purely instinctive manner we are not caught up in the inexorable but innocent existence of the animals, but in an ever-increasing isolation from the whole cosmos of living beings. We become auto-erotic. This no animal can ever be.

The quest for a purely animal sexuality makes a man the prisoner of his own Ego, cut off from nature and his fellow men, and from the Self he has it in him to become.

This drama of human choice is present in the puberty crisis. The boy cannot understand what is involved. It would be useless to try to show him the roots of his problem. He has to *live* the mystery of freedom. We cannot help him, at least at first, by expounding a philosophy or a theology. Yet we dare not be satisfied with the role of spectators of his agony—"We have been through all this and what fine fellows we are now (but are we?)—he will get over it in time. If there is anything we can do, it had better be to distract him as much as we can from his troubles." So we bring forward the various activities which we hope will ease his burden—sport, entertainment, youth movements and the like. If the sexual tragedies of so many adult lives are anything to go by, our medicine does not seem very effective. Like a good many others, it is physic directed to symptoms rather than causes, it removes the unpleasant spectacle of obvious sickness rather than the germ which is at its roots. I believe the whole problem of masturbation should be examined in the light of the general development and experience of the adolescent and not as an isolated, disturbing, inevitable phenomenon about which we can do little or nothing.

The masturbation habit, I said above, gives the boy a sense of power and at the same time a feeling of isolation. This separation from others is experienced not only in the sexual field but in various departments of life. For many, adolescence is a time of misery. Not that they are constantly wretched. There are moments of unspeakable joy, yet the background of life is more often than not a universal anxiety, an *angst*, whose consequences seem to take a lifetime to overcome. We shall never be able to help the adolescent in his difficulties unless we have kept the memory of our own youth. If the problem of masturbation is to be faced young people cannot be segregated, handed over to youth organizers, clubs and institutions which gallantly attempt to shoulder a task which is incumbent on all.

In adolescence the harmful effects of segregation, which is one of the marks of Western culture, on the development of the personality and the evolution of sexuality are only too apparent. The rise of the "Teddy Boy" groups, of gangs of adolescents, is a feature of the new conditions in all modern cities, where conglomerations of dwellings have no organic or traditional social focus (the community centre is an artificial creation), and young people are driven to form real groups of their own.

The feeling of isolation, then, drives the boy as he grows older to seek companionship. He comes to realize that he needs others if he is to emerge from the mysterious maze in which he finds himself. The prevalence of social segregation, the absence of true communities, force him to choose his companions among those of his own age and type. So common is this practice in every modern society that we tend to think it a natural phenomenon, and accept that youth can be happy only in its own company. Surely this is an illusion. Although there is a real sense of belonging to a particular generation it is wrong to imagine that this implies a wish to be kept apart from all others. The conflict of the generations, examined in a later chapter, is a genuine and necessary thing. Segregation makes its normal development and fruitfulness impossible. It forces the young to engage in the conflict by violence. They have to challenge their elders and the only way they can do this in our modern urban civilization is by the kind of conduct we label as anti-social. The teenage gang in its extreme form is the product of segregation.

The remarkable achievements of the Peckham experiment[1]

[1] A scheme carried out in Peckham, South East London, from 1935-39 and again from 1946-50. An account of its work is to be found in *The Passing of Peckham*, published by the Peckham Pioneer Health Centre, London 1951.

3

have shown that if young people are to develop healthily physically, morally and socially, they need the companionship both of those of their own age and of men and women of an older generation. As the body develops and muscular control becomes more assured, the boy and girl are initiated into sound physical skills—swimming, dancing, sports of various kinds—not by some paid instructor but by the people with whom they mix at the Centre. There are activities which require segregation of the generations and others which do not. The young learn from the old and then league together to challenge them in an atmosphere of friendly rivalry. But the Peckham experiment is an isolated case of genuine human realism. Most young people have to face their adolescence in far different circumstances. The coffee bar and the Palais de Danse are their special preserves. Here *"tant bien que mal"* they exorcize the devil of solitude by noise and obscenity. The beat of the jazz drum and the wailing of the crooner are fitting symbols of the sense of imprisonment and the longing for freedom which the adolescent experiences. We should not be contemptuous of all this. We have created the situation which makes it inevitable.

For a time at least, the young man and woman can find no solace in the life of the family. It has already been suggested that at this stage of development they need to be weaned from the womblike existence of childhood completely and for good. It is only when they can stand on their own feet that they can return to the family and see it for what it is, the supreme and irreplaceable institution founded on the unselfish love of its members for one another, the matrix of that intersubjective relationship which is the mark of true maturity. It is precisely at this critical moment when the adolescent has lost his family bearings that the community as a whole must step in to help him through the tortuous ways among which he now finds himself. It is in that larger community that his sex life should reach its own full development and lead him to his vocation of parenthood. The responsibility incumbent upon society as a whole is real and great. If it refuses this responsibility the young are driven either to the closed circle of their own groups or to inner isolation. In both cases, their personalities and their sexuality will emerge warped and unable to take up the tasks of adult life.

If our children are to grow into the independence which will make them capable of becoming true fathers and mothers in their turn, it is essential that they should be psychologically weaned. If they continue to seek refuge in the womb of the family, they will never achieve the family's final purpose, which is genuine manhood and womanhood. The adolescent may and often does live through his puberty crisis without having resolved the infantile complexes which make him too dependent on the mother. When he is driven into the larger community he will tend to seek some form of security which will take the place of the maternal womb. It is only in the community itself that he can find this security in a healthy form. If society is sound it will offer him responsibility in plenty, "a habitation and a name", duties as well as rights and privileges. He will learn from life itself to stand on his own feet, to play his own part in the whole pattern of society. If the community fails to offer him this opportunity, it easily becomes a substitute for the mother or father. If for the mother, then he becomes one of those sheeplike, unthinking citizens who never think or act for themselves, who expect the nation or the government to provide everything necessary for life. He will believe all he reads in his favourite newspaper. His sex life will be that of an undeveloped adolescent. Out of fear of trouble, he may remain physically faithful to his wife —and she herself will probably never know the full joy of adult sexual union—but he will enjoy the vicarious sexual delights of the smutty story and the suggestive novel, film or play. If he sees in the community, however unconsciously, a father substitute, he will tend to be one of those who are always "agin the government". He will become morose or envious of others, always insisting on his rights. Either he will treat his wife as a reincarnation of his mother and expect from her all the care and spoiling he received in childhood or he will guard her with all the jealousy his pent-up complexes can muster.

It is obvious that these considerations bring up the whole thorny question of work in the modern world and its effects upon personality. It is no use to long for the days of the craftsman. It is equally absurd to close our eyes to the immense personal problems work in our society raises at every stage of our growth. Most boys and girls leave school at the age of fifteen and are thrown into the amazing economic and industrial chaos of our times. It will seem odd to many readers if I suggest that sexuality is gravely affected by the kind of work we do. I am nevertheless convinced that this is so.

The modern factory offers little or no scope for the exercise of true responsibility. The function which should become the mainspring of adult life is unable to bite into the machine-minding task which the lad has to undertake. He is forced to look for other material on which to direct it. In the past, the trade union or the political party offered an opportunity both for psychological growth and for that entry into a larger and adult community which the adolescent needs. The emergence of the working class as a responsible section of society gave him the chance of growing to maturity by devoting himself to the welfare of the men and women with whom he worked. Nowadays the situation is very different. The working class has emerged, the Welfare State is established. Other and far less reputable communities attract the young. Most of these are brittle associations based on such things as financial interests. To be able to keep up with the Jones's has become a mark of status. Money has become the sign of social standards. The grammar school pupil, still busy with his books, feels inferior to his secondary modern companion who has left books behind and is now earning a good wage. The girl who works in an office is able to afford luxuries denied to the hospital probationer or the university student. Value is calculated not on personal qualities but on possessions. It is what you have rather than what you are which decides your place in the community.

The influence upon sexuality of this false attitude to the realities of life has some profound and obvious effects. In the past there were sexual initiation ceremonies in many factories. They were abominable and obscene but they did spring from a true if distorted and debased notion that, once a boy had left school and begun work, he was entering the sphere of adult life and responsibility. They are rare now, yet nothing more healthy has taken their place. If the new worker no longer has to undergo their obscenities, he still has to endure the pin-ups on the walls, the language, the general atmosphere of sexual immaturity just at the time when he should be leaving puerilities behind. Yet such an atmosphere seems inevitable. The work itself, less demanding than the craftsman's was, is also much less absorbing. The less developed functions, remaining immature, urge men and women to seek some outlet for their vitality in thoughts and activities which are still outside or free from the domination of the machine. And sex is the chief of these. The moral problem of work in an industrialized society needs far more attention than it receives. It is not enough to blame the depravity of the workers. The character of the work itself and of the artificial community which it produces is so inhuman that we may well understand the relief some moralists feel at the prospect of widespread automation and the possibility of a Leisure State. But these, too, will present problems.

One of the most striking features of work in the modern world is the manner in which it throws men and women together in the office, the shop and the factory. It is easy to be complacent about this and to argue that as both sexes have to live together there is no reason why they should not work together, that nothing will be gained by keeping them apart and since the realities of life cannot be avoided it is better to face up to them. Mixed schools, mixed society in the places of work are the order of the day. This point of view would be valid enough if the realities were genuinely faced. But are they? Sexuality is a force of tremendous power, and, until by love it is directed upon one person, it can ravage the personality, often beyond repair. If the work itself were an integrating process there would be little to fear. Where it is not, the way is open for disintegration which will be especially virulent in the sexual sphere. The adolescent is facing the great challenge of his lifetime, a challenge rooted in this emerging sexuality. The sectionalized, departmental, atomized society in which he has to live and work is totally inadequate to meet his needs. To imagine that he will be able to cope with the facts of sex merely by working with women in the factory is a singularly naive evasion of the real problem.

Inevitably I write from a masculine standpoint. Nevertheless it is necessary to say something of the puberty crisis as it affects the girl. It is difficult for a man to deal with this important stage in her growth since he has no primary consciousness of any form of sexuality other than his own. Yet certain aspects of the woman's development are common knowledge. The most obvious are the physical phenomenon of menstruation and the psychological phenomenon of female vanity. Menstruation links the woman far more profoundly to the whole cosmic process and purpose of sex than does any male sexual experience. From the onset of the menstrual periods the girl is brought into regular contact with the facts of generation under one at least of its aspects, since menstruation arises from the formation of ova in the womb. The man has no such direct and automatic relation with the formation of the spermatozoa. He is conscious only of the urge to expel them. And the final purpose of this expulsion is the impregnation of the ova. There is thus a fundamental difference between male and female sexual pleasure, both at the puberty stage and later. The expulsion of the blood and the unfertilized ova during menstruation has the opposite function from that of the emission of the spermatozoa. The latter is directed to fertilization of the ova, the former is the consequence of their non-fertilization. And no pleasure is experienced during menstruation.

In a subsequent chapter we discuss the precise nature of the female in conjunction with the problems of married life. In the present context, it must be noted that there is a divergence of opinion on this matter among sexologists. Some consider that sexual pleasure in the female is a psychical happiness at being possessed by the man, a general feeling of well-being and satisfaction, a euphoria rather than a physical orgastic sensation. On the other hand, orgasm can be achieved by the excitation of the clitoris or by the penetration of the vagina, and in many cases by both. At the puberty period large numbers of girls fall into masturbatory habits and produce auto-excitement and orgasm, although they are often unaware of anything reprehensible in these practices, and it may even be doubted whether they consciously connect this activity with their sexuality, which is so deeply rooted in their generative function properly so called. In any case, female orgasm seems to be very different from that of the male. His sensory eroticism is localized in the sex organs and not diffused throughout the body as in the case of the woman. Although her orgasm may have no immediate *primary* relation to the essential biological purpose of sex, its importance from the psychological standpoint is very great indeed.

The crisis of puberty brings the girl face to face with the mystery of sex as a creative force, the mystery, too, of a shared pleasure, having its roots in the soul, in the conscious realm of the love of the spirit and yet destined to be incarnated in the pure but physical gestures of the husband who will be the father of her children.

It can be said in conclusion that in both man and woman the crisis of puberty reveals the greatness and the weakness of our race. If this is so, then sex plays a part here which has no parallel whatever in the lives of the other animals. To us it reveals the mystery of our nature, our uneasy incarnation, our tendency to separate subject from object. In the most profound and spiritual sense, it shows us that we are naked. Body and passion should be clothed with the liberty of the spirit, though in fact they are exposed to the winds of impulse and instinct, healthy and fruitful in the beasts, disastrous in man unless and until they are assumed under the rule of freedom into the integrating processes of the primary consciousness.

IV

Falling in Love

WHAT IS the basis of that attraction which makes a young man fall so deeply in love that he is prepared to undertake all the responsibilities of marriage for the sake of the young woman of his choice? Among the other animals sexual attraction brings male and female together for mating purposes. This fact does not get us very far, for the mysterious thing about our own courtship is not the attraction of one sex for the other but of one individual person for another. Other creatures too mate in pairs and remain for a shorter or longer period together. We are unable to say how they choose their partners or even whether they do actually choose in any real sense. With human beings the element of choice clearly enters. Modern medical and psychological research, to say nothing of the fashionable philosophies, have accustomed us to the truth that our actions are far more conditioned than was once thought. Freedom with us is not the absolute liberty of choice our fathers took it to be. At the same time exaggeration in the opposite direction must be avoided. The data of the secondary consciousness should not make us draw hasty conclusions about those of our primary awareness. The experience of certain Eastern ascetics seems to show that a good deal of the conditioning of our freedom is the result of an insufficiently high and developed level of consciousness. The more conscious we become of the hidden forces in our own personalities, the less will our relations with ourselves and with others be conditioned by compulsions which are so powerful because they are unconscious. We are aware of freedom. We are aware of conditioning. To deny either is to impose a doctrinaire construction on our experience.

In the matter of attraction, individuals vary greatly. Dr Brétéché of Nantes (*Comptes rendus du XIIIe Congrès Français de Gynécologie*)[1] tabulates the results of his research into the different reactions of individuals towards the marriage act. He even attempts a classification of individuals into categories. Our own concern here is with the period that precedes marriage but we may admit that some kind of temperamental variations such as Brétéché noted are likely to affect the process by which a person is attracted towards another of the opposite sex. Ideally, Brétéché states, an individual in a particular category should find his or her partner in the same category or a similar one. There will then be a good chance of harmony in the married relationship, at least in the physical and to some extent the psychological sphere. Yet here, as elsewhere, the play of psychic forces and the pressure of social conditions complicate the situation and influence the choice.

This does not mean that we have no knowledge at all of the way in which physical attraction operates among human beings. We are well aware of the importance, for instance, of physical appearance. We know too that of itself this is a very shaky foundation for a lifelong partnership. Yet it is a fact that, to the young man in love, his fiancée appears beautiful however plain she is considered by others. It would, I am sure, be false to argue that he is blinded by his love, that he is being driven willy-nilly by an instinct whose urge he is disguising as a respectable response to the beauty of his future bride. It is surely the other way round. As Dr de Greef writes:

[1] Expansion Scientifique Française,, Paris. For details of Brétéchés categories, see below, p. 89, note 2. It should be borne in mind that there is no statistical confirmation of Brétéché's classification, and that it is put forward by the author simply to give some understanding of the complexity of individual variations in personality and response to situations.

"The genesis of the notion of the beautiful, obscure as it is, seems to us to be bound up with sexual differentiation" (*Médecine et Sexualité*, p. 72)[1]. In the same paper he points out that the process by which we acquire a sense of beauty also reveals to us the idea of value. Beauty, he says, demands an attitude of adoration in the psychological meaning of the word. We stand in awe and contemplation before what is beautiful. We are drawn away from love of self and caught up in the existence of what we contemplate.

In the period before puberty the sense of the beautiful remains more or less submerged in the unconscious. We are surrounded by the beauty of the universe but are not aware of it as a transcendent value. At the adolescent stage, like Caliban, we become conscious, however dimly, of the fact of beauty. For most men, it is the beauty of women which opens our eyes. It even seems that our whole attitude to the beautiful is largely determined by the physical and psychological forces set free in us by the sexual impulse as it urges us towards marriage.

As this is not a philosophical treatise there can be no question here of discussing what beauty is in itself; it will be enough for our purpose if we realize something of its implications. We experience a certain illumination of the mind in the presence of things or persons and we describe its cause by the term "Beauty". The experience itself is not merely an illumination, it is also a fascination. We are drawn to "the other" by some quality, some value in it. Ledoux's three degrees of relation are relevant again here. If there are three ways in which we may be related to all that is not ourselves, if we may be absorbed in the universe as in a womb, stand over against it as an empire to be conquered, or become consciously one with it, neither dominating "the other" nor sinking our own personalities into that of others, then the encounter with beauty represents the sudden setting before us of the immense

[1] Editions Spes, Paris, 1950.

value of others, of their subjective autonomy, of the attitude of "adoration" which we must adopt in their presence. Beauty, in a word, points beyond itself. The fact that there are differences of opinion as to whether a thing or a person is beautiful tends to confirm this doctrine.

A woman, a picture, a poem, a symphony will be beautiful for some and not for others. It is often held that "beauty is in the eye of the beholder", that *"un paysage est un état d'âme."* Obviously any relation implies a two-way traffic. Yet it would go counter to experience to suggest that, when two men see the same woman for the first time and one says she is beautiful while the other does not, the one who admires her is projecting some content of his unconscious mind onto her, and no more. If we hold the traditional view that all things that are have a kind of bloom upon them, an aspect of being which can and does fascinate, then everything is in some sense beautiful.

Sexuality, therefore, as it evolves in man, places us—particularly at the adolescent stage and at the time when we begin to think of marriage—in direct contact with the being of others as revealed to us by beauty and especially by the beauty of women, which becomes for us the archetype of beauty itself. Our Western sensibility is rooted in the love of women. In the arts which depend upon movement, the drama, music, the ballet, there is a remarkable parallel between the development of the work and the sexual play of courtship and intercourse. There is a series of minor climaxes all leading to the major climax, which is followed by a return to rest and silence. There is no reason to be horrified at this. On the contrary. The generative function of the animal, which already in the higher species has led to the exquisite ballet of courtship, is assumed in the human race into the world of the transcendental, the conscious world of the other seen as Being and as Beauty. And by a reverse process, the sense of the beautiful which our developing sexuality arouses in us is projected onto the whole universe of things. The beauty of women to which our developing sexuality draws our attention and under whose fascination it forces us to an act of contemplation becomes the principal matrix of our Western arts. This may be one reason why the great painters, poets and composers have usually been men.

The young man's sexuality awakens in him this sense of beauty to guide him in his choice of a partner. But the temptation of Don Juan is always with us. The free world of the spirit may be cut off by the mists of lust. Lust is desire divorced from ultimate purpose. It marks a fixation in the ego-centred state of the second, objective, tyrannical degree of relation. We may fail to see the reality, the being, the person, beneath the veil of beauty. We may fail to do this because, as de Greef suggests, our education and training has been of the sort to "desexualize art". Femininity, as he writes, may then "disappear in a complete disincarnation and so a massive sterilization of youth is brought about, so that when a man finds himself at length face to face with the conscious problem of sexuality, he has already lost the habit of submitting to authentic values, of submitting to value as such" (*op. cit.* p. 76). This failure to face reality may lead us into sexual disorders during and after adolescence. But we may fall into these for another reason. We may have given full rein to our sexuality, to our desires. We may be satiated with sexual experience of the Narcissus type, contemplating our own image in the bodies of others, never conscious of their reality, needs or destiny. We have become immured in auto-eroticism and are unable to see any values other than the immediate satisfaction of our own desires. We have failed to see the values our sexuality is to incarnate. We have failed to place ourselves in that attitude of "adoration" of "the other" which our consciousness imposes upon mankind. It is not for nothing that our fathers taught us to speak of "falling in love". We must indeed fall from the high, desolate peak of self-worship into the light and warmth of the world of "the other", the universe of the real, of the beautiful, of Being itself.

A too narrow conception of the term "physical attraction" must be avoided. It would be wrong to see in it nothing more than an animal drive to copulation. That drive is present, but it is not separable in man from the dialectic of consciousness, personality, beauty, love, being. The physical attraction which leads to marriage is in most cases only the substream of the growing consciousness of being under its aspect of the beautiful. A young man judges a woman beautiful and falls in love with her. However defective her beauty by any absolute standard, enough is revealed to him to draw his sexual forces into the orbit of the I-Thou relationship. However far he may move in his married life from this first intuition of the value of a person as glimpsed through her beauty, however aware he may become of the failure of that beauty to retain its fascination for him, yet it remains a fact that the initial experience of falling in love meant far more than the opportunity of unrestricted indulgence in sexual intercourse. It was essentially a great metaphysical revelation, an encounter with a person, a vision of a new realm. Such a revelation may have been imperfect. All kinds of maladjustments, sociological influences, defects in upbringing and education, may and do restrict the scope of this primary vision, but they cannot entirely destroy it. A man's fatherhood springs not merely from his sexual organs but from the fullness of his being. It is to this fullness that the vision of "the other" in the woman he loves calls him. He is to be the father of *persons* by union with a *person*.

What then is falling in love? What are the mysteries underlying the words "I give myself to you"? In the answers to these questions, in so far as they can be found and uttered, we shall find the final direction, the ultimate destiny of sexuality as it emerges from the purely biological plane on to that of human relation.

We have to remember that it is possible for people to fall

in love or at least to feel the impulse to do so at any period of life. The married are not exempt from this hazard. It is commonly argued that divorce is justified because love has absolute rights, and that if a man ceases to love his wife and finds he has fallen in love with another woman, the marriage should be dissolved and he should wed the person he now loves. This view is examined in a later chapter. It cannot be brushed lightly aside, for it raises ethical problems that can only be faced squarely at a more advanced stage in our discussions.

One further observation: it is all but impossible for me, as a man, to write of this experience from the woman's point of view, for few men have Racine's insight into the feminine soul. My remarks here are limited to the man's reactions. If this book prompts a woman to publish an essay similar to this, I shall be the first to welcome it.

The first characteristic of falling in love is, then, a sense of fascination. The phrase "He can't keep his eyes off her" expresses well the state of the lover. He is alone in the crowd until the loved one comes. He is lost in a kind of anonymity until she speaks to him. Her face is a light shining in darkness. When she is there, nobody else is of any importance or significance. Fascination involves a fixation. The psychologist will compare it to magic and suggest that there is far more here that the attraction of one woman exercising its power over a man. Is it not the story of Narcissus all over again? Is the woman any more than a mirror in which he sees his own image? Is it not the image he loves? The truth must surely lie deeper. The man is brought into contact not only with his own feminine side but, by the same token, with femininity itself. His own Anima is an image of Woman as such. The girl he loves is not merely the mirror of his unconscious self, she is also the symbol of womanhood itself. The fascination-experience leads in two directions. It opens the way inwards to the man's own depths and outwards to the world of the other sex as incarnated in this woman. It initiates a new relation in both the inner and the outer worlds, a new relation with the self and with "the other".

Normally the stage of fascination leads to a further stage, to that of uncertainty and anxiety. Will this love be returned? This anxiety arises from the desire to be accepted, the desire for a new and acknowledged relation. Already the Anima projection begins to give way before the objective problem of future status in regard to *this* woman. A critical choice has to be made. A man must speak or remain silent and so give up all hope of a love returned. But to declare his love means to tear apart the veils that hide his secret longings. This is not easy. There is a danger too. He may be rebuffed, refused. So long as he is silent, hope remains. Once he is refused, there is nothing left to hope for. Shall the risk be taken, shall he admit to a human being like himself that his happiness lies in her hands, that he feels only half alive if she will not consent to share his life? It is one thing to confess it to himself, but quite another to confess it to her, to make a kind of semi-public acknowledgement of his desperate need for relations with another person if he is ever to be complete.

If he is accepted, the engagement is announced. His choice is made, his love declared. The acceptance is symbolized by the kiss. The body already begins to share in the new relation. The woman is already preparing to give herself to her husband. During the period of engagement there should be time and opportunity for the couple to base their relationship on a far surer foundation than the initial attraction. The partners should begin to see one another as "subjects" to be loved for their own sakes. At this essential and critical stage, it may become obvious that there is no genuine love between them and that the experience has been in fact no more than an unconscious projection. It is as well that this should become clear before and not after marriage. If the engagement follows its normal course, the two families concerned will have some influence on the progress of the courtship. Yet on the whole, particularly in our own times, there will be little genuine contact between the future "in-laws" on both sides and the young people. The latter will try to get away together from both families for a few hours every day. This is understandable, but I believe that it is often carried too far. In the past, the business of marrying their children was taken more seriously by parents. This of course led to grave abuses, among which the "*mariage de raison*" has a specially bad name, which it did not always deserve.

The profound existential forces involved in the situation are well brought out in Thornton Wilder's play *Our Town*. Just before the wedding in the second act, each of the young people experiences a violent revolt against the other. They are about to risk everything on the faith and loyalty of another person of whom, after all, they know very little. The unknown opens like a chasm before them and they long to rush back to the security of the home and family in which each was born. In both cases, one of the parents gently leads them to the point at which courage returns and the leap into the future is taken with confidence and joy. The insight of the dramatist reveals here the inner nature of the act of choice at this moment of crisis. It is not only the young couple who are involved. Their movement onwards together is not only a personal matter for each of them, it is also a crucial matter for their two families. Their future existence depends at least in part upon this marriage. But the betrothed must break away from the family life they have known if they are to build a new home which shall be a guarantee of the survival in time of both stocks. The revolt against such a severance may remain buried in the unconscious. It is there all the same and active in the depths. Sooner or later, it will emerge at moments of strain or anger and one or other or both of the partners will look longingly back to the existence they knew before their marriage.

At his juncture, therefore, the existent families appear as the agents through which the necessary courage is made available for the new family which their children intend to found. If life is to continue in another generation, sacrifices must be made. The ceremonial rites at the wedding, in particular the giving away of the bride by the father, are symbols of the reality contained in the situation. The onward movement of the generations is usually made evident in the establishment of a new home in another house. The problem of housing is therefore not merely one of accommodation, but of vital importance to the new relationship which marriage produces. Questions such as these and others like them should be to the fore during the engagement period. Nothing in such a solemn event and state as marriage should be left to chance. The time before the ceremony should be thought of as a kind of noviciate during which the young couple discuss, plan and face together all the duties and obligations, as well as the joys, of their future union.

It is only too obvious that this serious view of the engagement period will not commend itself to many of our contemporaries. The objections which, even if they are not raised, are implicit in the lives of many engaged couples must be met, for they are constantly brought face to face with choices of the greatest importance not only for their own future but for that of their children and of the community at large.

First, the physical implications. In a sense the genital urge in men is more or less undifferentiated and promiscuous until the decision to marry is made. This does not mean that promiscuous sexual intercourse itself is inevitable before marriage. The sexual code of the community largely determines whether companionship between young men and women shall or shall not be physical in the fullest sense. As has already been pointed out there is a variety of customs in this respect among primitive peoples. Some forbid all pre-marital relations, others tolerate or even encourage them. Among Western nations there is now no absolute code. Much depends on the family in question. In countries where prostitution is common, young men—if not young women—often lead lives of considerable promiscuity. It is impossible, in view of the variety of character and of psychological stresses in different individuals, to determine how far such intercourse is solely the result of lust or of a genuine desire for love and a truly human relationship. At first sight, it seems to be an obvious example of fixation, if only temporary, at the second degree of relation. The partners, venal or otherwise, are treated as mere objects of pleasure, even where such pleasure has genuine metabiological implications.

The fact remains that many young men obtain sexual experience before marriage and in the majority of cases with professional or amateur prostitutes. The existence of prostitution is often justified by the virtuous mother on the grounds that it offers a safeguard for her daughters who might otherwise become the victims of the passions of men. She expects those they marry to remain faithful to their wives, and in the main, they do. Some of them become admirable husbands. They have sown their wild oats and now are content to be respectable citizens. Their wives may even benefit psychologically from their partner's previous "experience". The technique of conjugal love-making is sometimes learned in the brothel, though it seems appalling when the community at large is satisfied to leave instruction in this important aspect of married life to women who are mere objects of passing pleasure. Yet it is by no means certain that the "experience" so gained will automatically enable the husband to give his wife full satisfaction in intercourse.

If the young man has led a pure life, in the ordinary sense of the word, he will meet a different set of problems during his engagement. Quite soon he becomes conscious of physical desire. The kisses, embraces, caresses exchanged, lead to the erection of the penis. This purely reflex movement is obviously the preliminary to more intimate physical relations culminating in coitus. It is unfortunately true that many young women who have no intention of anticipating marital union are unaware of this phenomenon. Their ignorance may have disastrous consequences. While some men are temperamentally well able to control the desires which the body prompts, there are others who can only do so with the utmost difficulty. In some classes of society the dangers of indiscriminate exchanges of token of affection are taken so seriously that the young people are forbidden to indulge in them save within strict limits and more or less under supervision. On the other hand, most families, in England at least, show a wide tolerance in this respect. It is even argued that the young people have to accustom themselves to the physical side of their coming union. They must learn the art of self-restraint here and now and the only way they can do so is by going to considerable lengths and then calling a sudden halt before full intercourse is achieved. This idea might have something to be said for it if it were true that all men possess the same temperament and a high degree of medullary control. The opposite is undoubtedly the case.

The erectile tissues of the sex organ in the male produce a rapid tumescence in civilized man. The prevalence of all sorts of genital stimuli in Western Europe and America can lead to the destruction of the very idea of marriage and of the marriage act as an art to be practised with all the skill, humility and attention to the needs of "the other" which the artist and the craftsman bring to their work. Today, sexual intercourse is increasingly considered as a reflex, compulsive activity beyond genuine human control. Man is, so to speak, caught up in a sexual conveyor belt and, once involved in its unceasing movement, there is nothing he can do but allow himself to be carried along until the urge leaves him at the onset of detumescence. Among primitive tribes and the civilized East such a desperate and fundamentally inhuman conception of sexual intercourse and of our powerlessness to control it is looked upon as a sign of weakness and deficiency in manly strength and accomplishment.

It is against such an adolescent background of immaturity that most young people have to live through their engagement period, to say nothing of their subsequent married life. It would be most unwise therefore to be dogmatic about the kind and extent of affectionate manifestations at this time. What is really the point at issue is the training and education needed to prepare engaged couples for marriage. Once again, it must be emphasized that there is need for a new sexual "climate". There are signs of an awakening sense of the responsibility that falls on all. The business of training young people for marriage is the family's affair, no doubt, but what can a parent do to help his children at this fateful period of their lives? He cannot alter the climate of sexuality in the world today although, if he has seen his own sexual vocation from the standpoint adopted in this essay, he will have been able to do something to provide a more healthy sexual environment in the home. Nevertheless, he will know that marriage raises issues of great delicacy at both the spiritual and the physical levels. He may feel reasonably confident that his own child knows what he or she is about to undertake, but can he be equally sure of the partner who has been chosen? A father, for instance, may be on sufficiently good terms with his son to talk frankly with him, but the son's future wife also needs help and advice. If neither of her parents can face this task, who is to give her the guidance she should have? This is not a rhetorical question. This kind of situation is so common as to be almost the rule. Those who give their time and energy to the work of the Marriage Guidance Councils know that many of the problems they are asked to deal with would probably never arise if young people were properly prepared for marriage. To meet this real need, instruction courses for engaged couples are organized and men and women qualified to do so discuss with the young people the implications of their future life together at every level. Such methods are admirable. It is no argument against them that only those attend who are already well on the way to achieving true happiness in their married life. We all need help in deepening our sense of what sexuality is and involves.

Like all other forms of intellectual and moral training, sexual education must make a real contribution to human culture. I would even assert that a healthy sexual life is one of the finest kinds of education because it leads to that type of relationship between persons which ensures their maximum development and provides for their children the human climate they require if they are to be spared chronic adolescence, the endemic disease of our objective age.

The problem of the creation of an adult climate of sexuality remains the most urgent of all. No form of education, not even that of the good family, can do its work effectively if it has constantly to compete with an ever-increasing regression of society towards an unconscious, semi-instinctive form of life and thought. The school and the family cannot survive as educative forces if they are always to be islands of sanity in an ocean of absurdity. The urgent necessity of the revival of a genuinely human sexuality should be in the forefront of the preoccupations of all those, such as philosophers, scientists, clergymen, teachers, social workers and politicians, who will not rest content to see our civilization sink into a new and more terrible barbarism.

Many who are aware of the size and difficulty of this problem of education for marriage think that the modern mass media should be used. There is a spate of books, pamphlets and articles dealing with sex, and the cinema and the television have been brought into operation in the same cause. Yet anyone who writes on sex and marriage is disturbed by the fear that what is published will be read for quite other reasons and in a quite different spirit from those which have prompted the writing. The danger comes from the fact that sex can be and often is divorced from what is its true essence and purpose. It can be abused as a source of irresponsible pleasure. It can become the means of self-love and self-seeking. The great cosmic event, which intercourse essentially is in the human species, can be viewed as no more than a biological phenomenon and all its vital links with the development of personality and community may be severed. And this wholesale devitalization and dehumanization of sex is encouraged by certain people as a source of financial gain. In such an atmosphere it is little wonder that so many young couples come to marriage with hardly any conception of the grandeur of their vocation. It is not surprising that the number of broken and unsuccessful unions is vastly on the increase and that the divorce rate is reaching astronomical proportions.

In England, in certain sections of society, it is customary for young men and women to "keep company" with no avowed intention of marrying. They are allowed to behave like engaged couples and anything short of what is known as "immodesty" is tolerated. It is presumably argued that they will thus discover whether they are suitable partners for a possible marriage. In some districts a tradition even remains that they should have intercourse with the same object in view. What are we to think of this? The answer is surely obvious. When a young man makes love to a young woman he is conscious of sexual desire but, if he is really in love with her, of much more than just that. He is conscious of her as a person, as a subject with her own rights. This woman is different both from him and from all other young women. This personal differentiation is of enormous importance. If "keeping company" means anything at all, it will have to lead both parties to a knowledge of each other's temperament and character. Mere temporary love-making, however innocent, is hardly likely to bring about this fundamental confrontation. Boy and girl are too busy seeking pleasure, having what is called "a good time", either in the company of one another or in more general amusements, to bother about getting to know one another. This may seem a hard saying to many. Why should the couple not enjoy themselves? They will find life hard and grim enough later. It is no good trying to put old heads on young shoulders. They are too young to worry about character and temperament. Let them kiss and cuddle and when they have had enough of each other, begin all over again with someone else. So long as they do not get into "trouble", there is no reason why they should not flit from one association to another until the right man or woman comes along.

There are two grave objections to this plea. There is no guarantee that both parties to the love-making will be ready to break off the relation, such as it is. To one or other it may have been all the time, or have eventually become, a very serious matter indeed. A real and profound relation may have come into being, even though it is one-sided. Still more serious is the fact that if temporary love affairs or true engagements are to be no more than "good time" experiences, then the genuine problems will begin to rear their heads after marriage.

Some thinkers are so understandably obsessed with the difficulties which variations in temperament cause in sexual relations that they advocate which is known as "trial" or "companionate marriage". This is a more permanent and responsible form of the "trial" intercourse found in many rural areas. There is one important difference however. The country folk are chiefly interested in finding out whether coitus will produce pregnancy. If it does, then the marriage takes place. The advocates of companionate marriage have a wider view. They wish to avoid the breakdown in marriage which are proved to be due to sexual maladjustments or to profound psychological conflicts. As things are, they argue, these problems only emerge after the wedding. It is then too late to do anything but patch up a situation which should never have been allowed to arise. The couple have either to face a life of strain and misery or they must seek relief in separation or divorce. The problems raised by this argument are genuine enough and deserve careful consideration. I shall not attempt to retort by a mere statement of a moral code, even though I believe such an ethical approach is valid in itself, not least because it is rooted in the primary facts of human nature and relationship. The validity of the theory can be tested in the light of modern research into some at least of the causes of sexual maladjustment. Dr Brétéché, in the paper he read at Biarritz in June 1949,[1] expounds his theory of sexual classification. The information he gives is not easily available to the general reader. It may be objected that it is too frank, or that his conclusions are too sweeping for a book such as this. I cannot agree. I feel that the disasters which ruin so many marriages might be avoided were Brétéché's ideas more widely known.

He divides men and women into seven sexual categories[2] according to their reactions to the marriage act. As each type has physical and psychological characteristics which are fairly obvious, the value of Brétéché's classification for engaged and married couples is considerable. The complex nature of human love in its physical manifestations also

---

[1] See above, p. 74.

[2] Brétéché describes his seven types as follows:—the Solar, the Lunar, the Martian, the Venusian, the Jupiter, the Saturnian, the Mercurian.

In both sexes persons of the *Solar* type are tall and elegant, with limbs longer than the trunk. Their emotional reactions are limited but keen. They are liable to anxiety states, obsessions and phobias, are hyper-sensitive and very much on the defensive in their relations with others. They are often aesthetes, have inquiring, objective and conscientious minds. Their instincts are refined and delicate. The woman has no sexual initiative and must be approached with care and only at such times as she is prepared to co-operate. She must be aroused with great delicacy and loving attention. She must feel she is secure in her husband's affection.

Women of the *Lunar* type tend to be stout. Their reactions are weak in intensity but wide in range. They tend to live in a dream world remote from external reality. They have strong imaginations and good memories, but are only vaguely aware of the present and the actual. Physically, they are relatively insensitive. They have little interest in food, perfume, dress or personal cleanliness. Sexually, they give way easily but need some special circumstance to arouse them sufficiently for orgasm to ensue.

The *Martian* type is characterized by high development of the thorax and the limbs. The reactions are of a violent nature. There is a strong practical bent and much initiative. The Martian, as the word suggests, is a fighter and even a hero. The man is impulsive, often obscene and indecent. In coitus, he

leads to the points at which companionate marriage and the "trial" intercourse are seen to be quite inadequate to meet the problems they are supposed to solve.

Brétéché's categories, like all such schemes, are not water-tight. Few of us would recognize ourselves as belonging entirely to any one of them. Yet they point out an important truth and make us aware of the complexity of human nature and the great issues which are already beginning to appear on the horizon of the engaged couple. Brétéché, as a practising gynaecologist, receiving the confidences of his patients and, under a professional obligation to answer their questions and to help them to achieve that happiness in marriage which

acts rapidly, is egoistic and takes no time to prepare the woman. The Martian woman herself will often take the initiative in sexual relations. There is an obvious tendency to erotomania. Yet this is counterbalanced by frequent periods of sexual indifference, particularly if the physical energy is expended in other ways, in business, for instance, or sport. Since coitus is essentially egoistic for this type and has little relation to love, the Martian is often unfaithful and even feels little affection for his or her children.

Persons of the *Venusian* type have a highly developed trunk, thorax and abdomen. The fundamental psychological tendency is towards a mystical type of eroticism. The mentality is artistic. There is great sensitivity to harmonious design. The Venusian is musical, lazy, languid, a lover of the dance. In the art of love-making, the Venusian man is the most adaptable of all types, the most attentive to the needs of his partner, since his physical activities are firmly linked to his sentiments and feelings. He is in no hurry. He is the exact opposite of the Martian.

The man of the *Jupiter* type has keen and widely varying reactions. He is of a greedy nature and has a tendency to megalomania, is ambitious, a good organizer with a clear sense and appreciation of values, is able to think and express himself with ease and clarity. He is a man of order in both private and public life. He loves his home and is a model family man. He loves and is faithful to his wife and children, for he realizes and is proud of his family as being his creation. He is, in a sense, the typical *homme moyen sensuel*. In coitus he seeks to satisfy his wife and takes pleasure in her joy. The woman of the type needs strong, widely diffused caresses. Where both partners are of the Jupiter type, orgasm is quickly achieved and coitus frequent.

Men of the *Saturnian* type have prominent heads, necks and foreheads. Reactions are weak and restricted in range. There is a tendency to melancholy. The intellect is of the logical kind. The mind is critical, will reason about and discuss anything and everything. Reserved and lacking in enthusiasm, the Saturnian man is not sensual and will fall in love with difficulty. He has almost no instinctive life, no strong desires or impulses. He is quiet, clumsy and slow. In sexual relations, he finds no pleasure in the prelimin-

they rightly feel to be their due, has contributed another communication to the volume quoted above. Its title "Sexual education as the best prophylactic against anaphrodisia" reveals that he is no fatalist in this matter. Anaphrodisia, or frigidity, which implies the failure of the woman to achieve orgasm, is one of the most common and difficult problems of married life. It is not perhaps generally known that it is almost unheard of that a woman will desert a man who gives her full physical and psychological satisfaction in coitus. Marriage Guidance Counsellors will tell us that it is very rare for a marriage to break down where there is this mutual full relationship. They also know that it is all but impossible to per-

aries to coitus. Normally, his wife, if she remains faithful to him, will, in Brétéché's own words—"never know throughout her whole life the delights of an act during which he unconsciously remains egoistic and without any technical expertise". The reader of English literature will doubtless be reminded here of the story of Dorothea's relations with her first husband, Mr Cazaubon, in *Middlemarch*. The author observes the conventions of nineteenth-century English polite society and describes these relations without alluding to their sexual aspect. Nevertheless, we may read into the novel the obvious implications of the sexual problem, although George Eliot writes only at the psychological level. The woman of the Saturnian type is faithful but her fidelity cannot compensate for her lack of vitality in the sphere of the senses. Coitus is rare and she will be slow to reach orgasm unless her husband belongs for instance to the Jupiter class and so is prepared to do all he can to help her achieve it. She will be completely passive and unadaptable.

The *Mercurian* has large limbs, head and neck. His reactions are localized and he has a tendency to mythomania. He is inclined to ruse and self-centredness. He is eminently suited to life in great cities. His mind is receptive, he has wit and the grit of irony. He is adaptable, but capricious and unstable, alternating between moods of gaiety and fits of depression. He is sometimes exuberant, at other moments introspective. He passes from gentleness to attacks of bad temper. Physically, he is supple and adroit. In his sexual life, he shows great resource with the numerous partners his wayward passions lead him to approach on the sexual plane. His keen mental powers make him seek abnormal and vicious experiences during coitus. He may even become a masochist or a sadist. His desire for constant change, his love of liberty, his rooted egoism, tend to drive him towards a bachelor's life, where he is free of the responsibilities of a husband and a father. The Mercurian woman is an *"allumeuse"* rather than a person truly in love. She will be satisfied to marry for rank or money. She too is not usually content with one partner and proves an unfaithful wife. Her sexual adaptability has a very wide range.

suade a woman to return to her husband if she has left him because he is unable to satisfy her legitimate desires, and she has found another man able and willing to do so.

Such a diversity of temperament and characteristics as Brétéché describes may well make us wonder how any kind of *modus vivendi* can ever be achieved between a man and a woman. It should at once be obvious that a mere hedge-love coitus will give the lovers scant information about the various kinds of sexual behaviour to which their individual types give rise. Whether companionate marriage would be more successful in this regard will be considered in a few moments. For the present, we can confine ourselves to the question of how far are we bound by our type classification, whether our conduct in sexual matter is predetermined and whether any conscious effort on our part towards adapting our own kind of sexuality to that of our wives is bound to prove useless.

Brétéché makes it clear that a sound pre-nuptial education can modify the typological characteristics he describes. As always, it is the unconscious contents which do harm. Once we can see how our behaviour is influenced by the type to which we belong, we are on the way to freedom from compulsion in sexual matters. We can come to terms with ourselves. A young man must learn the general difference between the sexual requirements of men and women. He must also be made aware of the specific differences due to type variations. The general pattern in the case of the man, apart from typological modifications, is simple and well known. Desire is easily aroused, erection follows automatically and the preliminaries of coitus are all too easily seen as a way to achieve a speedy male orgasm. All that a man knows instinctively of sexual intercourse is concerned solely with his own satisfaction. Unless he is told, *he knows nothing of the needs of the woman.* In other words, Brétéché says in the terms of his own science what has been repeatedly insisted on in this book, namely that human sexuality is not a purely instinctive affair, which can be safely left to look after itself, but is indissolubly linked to the mystery of relation. Moreover, I suggest that, if the man is unaware of the woman's needs, it is equally true that the woman herself is rarely fully conscious of the implications of her own sexuality as far as coitus is concerned. Many wives will tell their friends that "there is no fun in it, only pregnancy". It is the duty of the husband to educate her not by lecturing her, which would be difficult during the engagement and cause great embarrassment, but by the manner in which, once they are married, he prepares her for coitus. This can be a thankless task, however, especially when there are strong repressions and phobias in the woman. And these are often due to a faulty upbringing and the fact that many girls are taught directly or indirectly to consider the whole subject of sex as "nasty".

We are now in a position to look at the claims made for companionate marriage. In the light of Brétéché's argument, it is clear that, though its advocates are facing up to a genuine problem, their solution is inadequate. The difficulties are serious enough where true marriage has been entered into. It is through a constant and sustained effort, particularly on the husband's part, to include the biological mechanism of sex within the higher purposes of relational existence, that there is always hope of achieving lasting harmony between the partners. The companionate marriage is based on a condition, and to condition a relation is to deprive it of half of its strength and reality. It is to begin with that egocentric, objective approach to "the other", which prevents intersubjective relations from emerging. To take a man or woman on approval is essentially inhuman. By apparently solving one element of the problem, we make the solution of the rest impossible. And, as was emphasized above in the case of couples "keeping company", what if one person is satisfied at the end of the probationary period, while the other is not? What too, if children are born during that time? It is no answer to say that the probationary intercourse would have to be contraceptive, for that would be to beg another question of still greater implications. Companionate marriage is based on the isolation of the physical, typological, psychological aspects of the union into separate compartments. There is an initial disintegration, a conditional fidelity, which is no fidelity at all, since a relation founded in an act of mutual faith involves of its very nature a total renouncement of self-seeking. This may seem a hard saying. It is, but human life is not an easy business. If we are to become what we have it in us to become, we have to accept the conditions which alone allow us to grow into complete persons.

In the matter of conscious control over physical reactions which we assume are radically reflex, the West has much to learn from the East and from such primitive peoples as Malinowski's Trobrianders. The degree of mastery over the body which other races can and do achieve suggests that we have neglected an important aspect of education. Among certain classes of Hindu, there is a remarkable control of what we consider purely automatic reactions. Of the Trobrianders, Malinowski says that their marital intercourse is marked by great self-restraint on the part of the man.

Herrigell's remarkable book *Zen in the Art of Archery*[1] describes the training of the Japanese archer. When the learner has reached the final stage of his art he is able to hit the centre of the target in total darkness and then to shoot another arrow which will transpierce the first one. The bow used appears at first to be so clumsy a weapon that the learner cannot believe he will ever be able to use it at all. Gradually he comes to see that the secret of success lies in the mind. By complete physical and mental relaxation, above all by a complete emptying out of all self-regarding anxiety and desire, he

[1] Routledge and Kegan Paul, 1953.

reaches a stage at which his whole being seems included in that of the arrow and is attracted with, by and through it into the Great Centre of which that of the target is only a symbol. Such a purification of the objective approach to the realities of self and others contains a lesson for the Western mind, engrossed as it is in the scientific project and the quest for a control of the physical world based upon techniques. The influence of these techniques upon personal relationships and the search for self-knowledge is profound and in many ways disturbing. The problem of intersubjective relationships—so critical in marriage and family life—is at the heart of the tragedy of Western culture. Nor need we look only to the East for light in dark places. Our own traditions contain treasures of doctrine and practice which we have largely forgotten and whose rediscovery would do much to restore a balance which has almost been lost.

There are other obstacles confronting the engaged couple who are taking their mutual promises seriously. One of the most serious of these has been well described by Gustave Thibon in his book *Whom God has Joined Together*.[1] He points out that in the past people always married within their own class. Nowadays we find unions between men and women of very different social, geographical and professional types. Thibon does not think that this is a sign of progress. Not, he argues, that no such marriage ought ever to take place, but that it should be the exception to the rule. He writes: "A prince can only marry a shepherdess successfully if she has the soul of a princess." Or, it might be added, if the prince has the soul of a shepherd. Where there are deep religious, cultural and national differences between the partners, their life together will risk complete breakdown unless each, or at least one, of them is of sufficiently strong moral calibre to accept many if not all of the values essential to the other. If they are isolated

[1] Hollis and Carter, 1952.

from one another in certain sections of their lives, the increase of mutual love will be impeded. Not that the wife of a Bach must be a great performer or composer. She should at least be an Anna Magdalena. It is true that there have been and are marriages in which the differences, although considerable, have led to a deeper union. St Thomas More's first wife was relatively uneducated and he became her teacher. In the case of international marriages, the traditions of two great nations may be so harmonized that the marriage enriches immensely the lives of husband, wife and children. But such a success is possible only if the partners are willing and able to make sacrifices beyond the ordinary run of those essential in every union. They must possess spiritual strength of a high and even exceptional order.

Not only physical and cultural variations need to be borne in mind; there are also the psychological differences which are of such importance in the sphere of personal relationship. Their potentialities for good and evil may be already apparent during the engagement period. They will certainly emerge in all their power after the marriage. Whatever validity Jung's theory of psychological Functions may prove to have, it is obvious that some such classification does exist and that it has deep repercussions in the realm of sex. If a wide variation in physical characteristics is, as Brétéché says, a major obstacle to happy marriage, a similar variation in the psychological sphere is equally so, although here again such differences may be the source of great enrichment where man and wife are strong enough morally to use them as a basis for mutual understanding and integration.

In the case of the man, and to a certain extent in modern times in that of the woman, business or professional life influences, however unconsciously, the development of the personality. Men of the same trade tend to adopt similar responses to the demands of life. We all know the schoolmaster who is always didactic, the doctor who sees every problem from the point of view of pathology and therapeutics, the scientist who applies his techniques uncritically to philosophical or political questions. The professional life imprints on us what Jung calls a Persona—a mask which is necessary if we are to succeed in our personal relationships at the professional and public levels but which often hides a welter of undeveloped, unconscious material in the psyche. We may too easily take the Persona to be the only pathway to reality and so be unaware of vast regions of our own and others' personalities. The neuroses of middle age are part of the price we pay for this negligence.

This problem is mentioned again in a later chapter. At the moment, its implications should be borne in mind during the engagement period, when the temptation to "have a good time" is so strong.

It may appear odd to the reader that this chapter should conclude with a brief consideration of another option facing young people of marriageable age, that of consecrated virginity. Yet this vocation is highly relevant to our argument, since it calls for a personal choice in which the whole question of sexuality and its purposes is deeply involved. The taking of a vow of perpetual chastity is a feature of many religions, including Christianity. The existence of the vow and all that it implies often causes those who intend to marry to wonder why their future state should be looked on as inferior to that of virginity. There is one immediate difficulty of terminology. The word "virginity" has a clear sense in the woman's case, where it means the renouncement of all sexual intercourse and experience of every type. In the case of the man, the medullary system automatically leads to periodical erection and ejaculation during sleep. Physical virginity in the strict sense is therefore an impossibility for him. The woman can remain physically a virgin. For the man, virginity can only mean the renouncement of fatherhood and all the conscious sexual acts which are directed towards achieving it.

This distinction is not so academic as it may sound, since some of the oldest arguments in favour of virginity are based on the value of physical integrity which obviously means virginity as it was defined in the woman's case. However, the relational facts in either case are the same. The virginal or celibate vocation is first and foremost the renunciation of fatherhood and motherhood and of the exercise of genital sexuality.

As this vocation is always linked to a religious system, its justification arises from doctrinal principles. These vary according to the religion. For the sake of clarity, here are two examples. The Buddhist attitude to virginity is the result of the Buddhist philosophy of life. The aim of the ascetic is to rise above perpetual involvement in the circular movement of the wheel of existence. The soul is doomed to successive reincarnations and can only find freedom from this bondage by a series of purifications which at length admit it to a higher spiritual realm. To father children is to bring into the world other persons who will be condemned to the wheel of life. To choose the vocation of virginity is to concentrate all one's efforts upon the attainment of the ultimate goal. This striving after release is not a self-centred quest. The would-be Buddha must not look upon his training in perfection as an entirely selfish and personal affair. He is counselled to seek perfection by also leading others in the same direction. Nevertheless, the doctrine of reincarnation does teach that at the birth of each child, a soul returns to the sad earth, for it is not yet fit to enter the paradise of Amitabha, "where the sweet sound of the doctrine never ceases". A man who renounces fatherhood not only raises himself in some sense above the wheel of life, but also brings nearer the great day when all living things will find release. This attitude does not imply that sex is evil in itself but it does suggest that all life, in so far as it is tied to the phenomena of change, is relatively evil. Therefore, the further we move from its inexorable processes by conscious mortification the better for ourselves and ultimately for all mankind.

The motives which determine a Christian to take the vow of chastity are of a very different kind. It is still possible, though less likely than it once was, that a young man may decide on this course because he thinks sex is an evil thing and that he will pass out of the sphere of its corrupting influence by means of the vow. Such a belief is thoroughly heterodox and no monastic superior or diocesan bishop would accept a candidate who holds it and is honest enough to say so. What is far more probable is that the man, through faulty upbringing and a misunderstanding of religious doctrine, may disguise his heresy under seemingly orthodox forms. He may deceive himself as well as others by so doing. He may persuade himself that he reveres the sacrament of matrimony but feels that he is called to a higher state. If this unconscious heresy persists, it is probable that nature will later assert her rights and a major tragedy may wreck his life.

Another motive may be sheer fear of sexuality as such or of the obligations of fatherhood. This is compatible with a theoretical appreciation of the value of marriage and its sacramental character. The fear of intercourse rather than of its possible consequences is more frequent among women than men. It may even result from an unconscious desire to find security in an institute which will provide security and cushion the novice against the trials and troubles of the world. Escapism can be the initial urge, for instance, in young girls who have been educated at convent schools, where the religious have instilled puritanical fears of sex into their pupils (this is easy enough to do quite unconsciously) at the same time providing them with every kind of comfort and happiness. This escapist attitude is seldom able to survive the stresses, strains and austerities of a well-ordered religious house. It may, however, give rise to a strong Animus fixation. The lives of celebrated nuns give ample evidence of the existence in communities of women of this urge to domination and power. Many a saint has had to contend with it in herself and among her sisters. It is one of the hazards of this vocation. Until the religious arrives at a true estimate of his or her sexuality and the part it must play in the religious life, the whole essence of the virginal vocation will have been missed.

The traditional theology of Christendom recognizes this vocation as superior to that of marriage, even though the latter is a sacrament of the Church while the former is not. St Paul teaches that a man or woman who is celibate will think primarily of his duties to God rather than of how to please the wife or husband. He makes it clear elsewhere that the service of one another in marriage is also the service of God. Celibacy is a higher state because it allows a more direct and untrammelled form of that service. Later theologians have given other reasons. Their teaching depends on the doctrine of the Fall and the deductions they make as to the nature of spiritual and physical life before the advent of original sin. St Thomas Aquinas, for instance, says that virginity in the state of innocence would not even have been a virtue. There would have been no lust, no self-seeking in sexual intercourse. If virginity is now so highly prized, it is because it removes a man or a woman from the domination of inordinate desire. He makes it clear that he does not confuse lust with pleasure. Pleasure would have been far more intense in the state of innocence than it is now. It is not the pleasure which is evil but the inordinate desire for it. A man who eats in moderation has just as much pleasure at his meals as does one who is greedy, but his desire does not dwell on the pleasure for its own sake.

For St Thomas, therefore, the essence of integrity surely resides in the will and the reason. In the state of innocence desire could be controlled and so never become immoderate. In the terms of the argument in this essay, the love of the other would dominate the love of self. Since the Fall, desire outstrips moderation and to a greater or lesser extent overpowers reason and will. The bodily activities in which this inordinate and unreasoning desire is incarnated are themselves outward signs of that inner loss of integrity, that proper command of the self, which are proper to a state of innocence. Sexual intercourse is one among many such activities. Asceticism, renunciation in all walks of life, are now part of the equipment we all need on our journey back to the original state of personal integration from which we have fallen.

To those who do not believe the Christian revelation, such teaching and its consequences seem absurd and undesirable. Yet it is improbable that the state of consecrated virginity, if it were absolutely and inherently absurd and contrary to human nature, would have survived for so long, still less would have produced so many superb examples of personal integration and vigorous vitality.

Virginity must be for the novice a vocation to integrity not merely for its own sake, as though it were a private possession. Here Christian and Buddhist doctrines agree. Virginity must be seen as a call to the practice of a more perfect form of self-giving than even marriage affords. Sexuality is not suppressed. If it were, psychological compulsions would result and enslave the novice to other disintegrating forces. Rather is sexuality assumed into another type of vocation, activity and dedication. Sex in man, since he is a conscious being, must be the sign and symbol of a true relation or it ceases to be human and sinks lower than that of the beasts, who are controlled by instinct. Virginity demands the sacrifice of the normal symbol of married relationship in favour of a lived and living symbolization of the union of man with the Great Source of all being and relation, and with all other men. The diocesan clergy, for instance, must devote themselves to their people as genuine fathers in God, if they are to be true to their vocation. As Jean Guitton has written, both marriage and consecrated virginity are states of oblation, and a deeper understanding by the married of the higher vocation of the priest, the monk and the nun reveals truths concerning the eminent dignity of their own state, of which they would perhaps otherwise remain unaware. The same is true conversely of those who "have become eunuchs for the sake of the kingdom of Heaven".

Ideally, and despite defects in practice, the fact of consecrated virginity, when seen as a genuinely sexual phenomenon at the highest level of personal sacrifice, is of immense value and importance to those about to marry and those who are already married. It does not, or should not, make them feel that their own vocation is only a second best, a concession to poor human nature as the phrase goes. On the contrary, it should show them that both the married and the consecrated virgin are on the same upward path of sacrifice and self-renunciation, loving at different levels.

What of those men and women who do not marry, and do not enter on a life of consecrated virginity either? Are they fated to be deprived of all the advantages of marriage and parenthood? We assume that the unmarried for the purposes of the argument are men and women who, either of their own free will or by force of circumstance, have no sexual relationships. The bachelor or spinster who indulges in more or less promiscuous intercourse raises other problems. In what sense, then, can the unmarried we have in mind fulfil their destiny of handing on the life they have received? Their case is not on a par with that of the religious celibate. Marriage and consecrated virginity are both examples of self-sacrificing love. The bachelor and the spinster have not sacrificed their sexuality in the interests of a wider love ... or have they? This is the crux. We have argued that sexuality in man is not merely biological. It is not simply an animal function. It marks both men and women in every aspect of their being, character and existence. Freud's doctrine of sublimation or, as we prefer to call it after Guitton, "assumption", is to the point here. Where the sexual activities cannot be exercised as symbolical of our love for others, the forces of love can find other outlets, other expressions, other acts by which they make relations with other persons both possible and fruitful. In marriage itself, the genital acts are by no means the only or, in some respects, the most important manifestations of love. Human life and consciousness, however profoundly marked by sexual differentiation, are not limited in the expression of this differentiation to the biological functioning of the sex organs. The unmarried may and do show their love for others by lives of self-sacrifice and service.

Nor must we forget that the parent-child relation does not exhaust the relational possibilities of family life. The unmarried are normally members of a family and may find work enough and to spare within its circle. Their detachment, however involuntary, from many of the stresses of family life can lead to fruitful relationships with their nephews and nieces, and they can serve as a link between the family and the outside world. To their professional lives the unmarried often bring the full force and energy of their sexuality in its sublimated form, finding deep satisfaction in their relations with their colleagues and in their work.

It must be remembered that to renounce the exercise of the physical forms of sexual activity does not of itself diminish the vital forces of mind and body. It can do so accidentally, where the lack of genital intercourse is or becomes a sign of the drying up of the springs of love in the soul. This barrenness is far more deadly than that of the body. The latter may be compensated for by spiritual fatherhood and motherhood. We have only to see the real affection and devotion shown to her patients by a hospital sister to realize that there is more than one way of being a mother. On the other hand, the sight of an old bachelor who has chosen this way of life because it allows him to do what he likes with little or no consideration for the needs or the feelings of others will reveal the appalling unfruitfulness of so self-centred an attitude for the personal development of the individual. Both instances have their counterparts in the married state. If there is one thing more

distressing to observe than a smug, self-satisfied, self-preoccu-
pied bachelor, it is a greedy, devouring mother who in her
self-love stifles the life of her children, seeing them just as
pegs on which to hang the projections of her own worship
of self. On the other hand, the devoted mother whose whole
aim and ambition is to lead her sons and daughters to that
point in their growth at which they can safely leave her to
make their own way through life, unafraid and full of a love
for all that is real and good, has her counterpart in the unmarried woman who gives herself to the service of others who
need her, and in them finds the children which have been
denied to her body.

V

The Family

THE BIOLOGICAL and psychological aspects of sexuality may be, and are, "objects" of knowledge; they can be isolated and studied as phenomena. It remains true, however, that their ultimate sense is only discovered in the realm of conscious relation. When we look at the family which marriage inaugurates we can no longer stay in the purely objective sphere. We cannot stand outside the family and judge it, for it contains us.

Nevertheless, an attempt must be made to consider those occasions in family life which bring the family's essence vividly into the consciousness. There are moments of crisis, moments of revelation when this essence stands clearly before and within us and can be seen for what it really is. It is not really surprising to find the family's essential being revealed in the work of novelists, rather than in the sociologist's text-book. It has already been suggested that one of the functions of art is to make us aware of those realities within ourselves and others which have subjective resonance rather than objec-tive meaning. The kind of situation which a skilled and sensi-tive novelist or dramatist is able to describe will recall similar moments of crisis in our own experience of life in the family to which we belong, as well as in that of others whom we know.

The initial crisis of the new family obviously arises when the engagement period comes to an end and the young couple find themselves together as man and wife. It is a commonplace that the attitude of the young husband to his wife during the honeymoon may make or mar their whole future life. In a book such as this, it is impossible to go into any detail concerning the truly human and loving intercourse which coitus should be. This has already been discussed as far as seems necessary for our purpose, but it must be emphasized that intercourse, like any other art, is not perfectly achieved all at once. It needs mutual understanding and tolerance on the part of both man and woman. It takes time to know the needs of another and to succeed in giving that satisfaction which is an essential part of perfect union. Nor is this easy. It would be absurd to expect a newly married couple to reach at once the stage of perfect harmony in this respect. Everything depends on the way in which the husband sets about his task. If his wife senses that he is doing his best to help her, she will, provided she really loves him, forgive his lack of skill. If, on the other hand, he takes possession of her as though she were a piece of property solely for his own enjoyment, she will receive a wound in the soul from which she may never fully recover. But young wives should know the facts of intercourse—the biological information alone is quite insufficient—so that they can in their turn help their husbands.

Young husbands often complain of their wives' frigidity. There are a small number of cases where this embarrassing symptom is due to organic or functional disease, but normally the cause lies in definite phobias from which the woman is suffering. These fears may be conscious or unconscious. Nowadays the dread of pregnancy is a common enough reason for their presence. Defects in or even a complete lack of sexual education is another.

The first task of the newly married is the building up of their own home. They have each had a different experience of domestic life. The habits and customs to which they have been used may cause serious clashes, and decisions have to be made. There is ample evidence—and all of us can provide it from our family histories—of profound estrangements caused by what seem to be trifles. Objectively, they are only trifles. Yet they represent a deep conflict between personalities. They should never be treated lightly. If a couple can come to terms over such apparently minor matters, they will have achieved a major victory over self-love. Under modern conditions, however, another difficulty, of the opposite sort, may arise. So many young people spend their leisure away from the home that, once they are married and the honeymoon is over, the prospect of staying at home with one another may be very bleak indeed. At first it may well be that they go to the opposite extreme and refuse to see any visitors. If this attitude should persist, as it sometimes does, we have the unhealthy phenomenon of the home shut in on itself, refusing its light and warmth to others who would benefit by them. It is far more likely that there will be a difference of opinion as to how evenings and weekends should be spent. Where the woman passes her day in the home, she will want to go out in the evening. The man has been away since morning and would be content to sit by the fire once his work is done. As many young married women now continue in employment, at least until the first child is born, another problem arises. The man, although glad for financial reasons that his wife is still earning, may be critical of her housekeeping. He may come from a family where everything was kept spotless and in order, and expect his wife to be as adept with the duster and the cooking as his mother was. In this respect, there can be no doubt that careful designing of flats and houses to avoid accumulation of dirt and dust and to make tidying a quick and easy operation have helped to some extent to prevent many a marriage from coming to grief: to say nothing of that admirable contraption, the pressure cooker. These are excellent examples of objective science serving the cause of intersubjective relationships.

One thing is clear: crises inevitably come and they show that the family, even in its simplest form as man and wife, is an educative force in the deepest sense of the word. It presents vital options, inscribed in the very stuff of life, which will lead to choices whose results on many lives may be incalculable. The whole future of the We-community is at stake. The marriage will either degenerate to a mere cohabitation from which all genuine intersubjective relationships have vanished; or it will grow into a union of souls and bodies, so vast in its scope that the children born of it will begin their own lives in an environment integrated and integrating, so that they will stand every chance of becoming integrated persons themselves.

During the early months of married life there are often complications due to outside influences. The grim figure of the mother-in-law is not entirely a creature of fiction. She represents both a danger and an opportunity. The older generation always and inevitably believes its experience has taught it wisdom and that it has a duty to hand this wisdom on to the next generation. This would seem legitimate enough. Yet there are objections. The larger family, in this situation where two generations confront one another, is itself faced with an option. If the older one forces its wisdom and the fruits of its experience upon the younger in the fashion symbolized by the domineering mother-in-law, where will be that spontaneity in the new generation, that direct coming to grips with reality which is the essence of life and of a living tradition? Will not the pressure of past experience, and the past is never exactly the same as the present, prevent the larger family itself from flowering in those new forms which the vital processes of a growth through time should themselves produce? On the other hand, if the young couple is to begin all over again from the start and take no advantage of the experience and knowledge of its elders, will not the result be substantially the same? Will they not find themselves at the end of their lives at the point their own parents had reached? Will not the process of family growth be held up by this attempt to start from scratch? In fact, there are no easy solutions to personal problems. No two situations in life are precisely the same. This book will have done its work if its readers are encouraged by it to put such questions to themselves in the context of their own family existence. The family offers us the chance of grappling with the real problems of human life far more effectively than does any other society, since these problems are inscribed in the bodies and souls of those who form the family community.

There is a tendency today to think that life's difficulties can only be discussed and resolved at the public level. Those who serve on radio and television panels or give advice in the glossy magazines are expected to have ready replies to queries over which a Plato or Pascal would have spent a lifetime of careful meditation. If family problems are solved by, with and through the relational pattern which is formed in the home, then the chances that they may be solved in the aspects at which they affect public life are proportionately greater. If they are not faced and solved in the home, there is little probability of their being solved elsewhere.

The truth of this contention may be seen from one example. State education in England, in spite of its undoubted success in the case of the small minority of children who are specially gifted, has failed to raise the general standard of culture over the past fifty years. This is admitted by all. The apparent anomaly is explained in various ways, but it is not sufficiently realized that the school cannot take over or be a substitute for the educative functions of the home. If personal relations, which are the true basis of genuine culture, are not developed and deepened in the family circle, there is little opportunity of developing them in the school, with its inevitable herd characteristics and its emphasis on objective knowledge. But when the family life is full and rich, the school's contribution to the growth of personality can, as was argued in a previous chapter, be of the highest importance and value.

Pregnancy and childbirth are events of great moment not only for the child but also for his parents. During the months before her confinement, the woman undergoes profound physical and spiritual changes. Here it is essential that the witness of a mother should be heard. We make no apology for quoting at length from a passage in Père de Lestapis's book, *Amour et Institution Familiale*.[1] It is from the pen of Madame Giard. She writes:

> We have lost the feeling that motherhood is, in the first place, a blind, creative force, placed in us by Providence to assure the permanence of the race. If we regain an intuitive and complete sense of the mystery of the race and its duration, we shall give back to motherhood its fundamental meaning as a magnificent source of life.
>
> During the months of pregnancy, the mother is already living with her child. Never will it belong to her more intimately, never will she be able to do more for it than during those months of intimacy. Her work is, of course, unconscious, but in doing it, the mother delights to think of the mystery of so complete a union. As the child leaps in her womb she feels that which comes from her gradually taking on its own rhythm and its own independence. *How deeply moved she is to witness these first evidences of an existence which is not her own and yet which is mingled with her own.* There is that little child within her, his head on one side, leaning on his shoulder in that solemn attitude which comes before birth. In appearance, he is an impersonal embryo and yet he carries all the potentialities of the race (pp. 136, 137. Italics ours).

This quotation is significant from both the psychological and existential points of view. Note the words "the sense of

[1] Editions Spes, Paris, 1948.

the mystery of the race and its duration". In Jungian terms
they may be translated "the realization of the unconscious as
the mystery from which consciousness rises and from which
it must ever enrich itself". And again: "She feels the life
which comes from her gradually taking on its own rhythm
and its own independence." As a person, the child is still unknown to her. It is still a mystery which will be revealed, and
then only partly, at its birth. Its life, still so intimately linked
with hers, is a symbol of consciousness itself, sleeping in the
womb of the unconscious, a symbol too of the great archetype
of the Eternal Child, the new, the pure, the mighty one, the
Prince of Peace, in whose presence the lion will lie down with
the lamb. He is still impersonal, yet he bears within him "all
the potentialities of the race". And involved also is another
figure, that of the Great Mother. Her own motherhood is not
yet limited, circumscribed, concentrated, as it will later be in
her conscious care for the newborn child. She is still the one,
unique Mother, in whom is present "the blind, creative force
placed in us by Providence to assure the permanence of the
race". If ever there were a situation in which a human being
is near to the Creator and most like him, it is surely that of a
woman awaiting the birth of her child.

For the husband, the archetypal experiences at this time are
far less vivid. He is concerned, as always, with the common
problems of every-day life. He has to think of the practical
economic factors which will come into play when he and his
wife are parents. Yet there should be an attitude of mind, a
conscious effort to enter into the vast experiences of the
mother, a tenderness and reverence in his treatment of her, a
wholehearted devotion to her interests and to those of the child
in her womb—all of which will have incalculable effects on
the development of his and her personality, on their mutual
love and relationship and on the character of the child. It almost seems as though Nature herself is aware of this, and in
her own peculiar way, and not without humour, sometimes

provides the husband with the means of sharing his wife's inner life at this moment.

Nevertheless, it is usually at the time of the child's birth that the experience of paternity comes fully to him. He then sees and handles what till then has been an object of faith. I am convinced that the modern custom of keeping the husband away from the wife during the confinement is a real abuse. The mutual joy, gratitude and wonder felt at this time by both parents can have profound psychological consequences, provided they are together. The danger facing the man is that he may identify himself with the Great Father archetype and become so inflated with a sense of his own importance as the social and economic head of the family that his own personality becomes warped. The physical experience of paternity, especially at the moment of the child's birth, breaks down this undesirable identification. He sees this little child lying at his mother's side. There rises within him a feeling of near-adoration in the presence of these two persons whom he loves. He has witnessed with his eyes the labour which is the price his wife pays for her maternity. He has done what he could to enter into it, to lessen its intensity, to share it. Even today, there is always the fear that death may intervene. Every confinement places man, woman and child at the heart of human destiny. But now, the pain and the fear are gone. There is only joy, peace and love. As he looks at the child, who is the fruit of that love, he realizes a whole new dimension has come into life. The Ego loses its inflation. The archetype is no longer the master but the servant and all its immense forces pour into the soul of the "little father" and so restore the balance which the struggle for existence may have disturbed.

This experience of fatherhood is linked with that of motherhood in his wife. Whereas the mother's first thought is for her baby, the father's includes both child and mother in one and the same upsurge of joy and gratitude. He knows when he sees the body of his child that love and life are one. It is through his wife and her new vocation that this supreme truth is revealed to him. Their whole relationship takes on a new and far deeper character. He now sees it is involved in a cosmic process far beyond the little world of the individual. Personality has infinite echoes.

The birth of the first child brings the problem of the home and of domestic life into focus. Obligations are now obvious and impelling, in particular for the mother. She is bound morally and physically to the child. Even in the rare cases where it is handed over to the care of a nurse, the love of the mother for it imposes real restrictions on her movements. For the father, too, there is a critical option. This new mother-child community contains immense possibilities for good and evil which directly concern him and demand that he should be aware of his own role in the drama which is being enacted. The future development of the child requires, as noted in a previous chapter, that the mother should not revert to the pre-natal identification with the Great Mother archetype. Then it was healthy. Now it would be the exact opposite. If she becomes possessive, if she allows her love for the child to become contaminated with the myths of the unconscious, then those dark, hidden forces, so good when issuing into conscious life, so evil when they remain as the unknown tyrants of the inner kingdom, will distort her relations with the child and so prejudice the chances of its own healthy personal development. The father and mother in the presence of such hazards must remain lovers, so that the child, instead of being overpowered by the love of one only of its parents, is caught up in the mutual affection of both. So are the great problems of humanity itself, of society at large, rooted in the soil of family relationship.

We must say a word here about childless couples, among whom we do not include those who deny themselves children of set purpose. We are concerned with men and women who have wanted to have a family but have been unable to do so.

Physical fatherhood and motherhood have been denied them. Has their sexual life therefore been without meaning and purpose? Have they failed to incarnate their love for one another? We answer both questions straight away in the negative. Sexuality is of itself biologically directed to the birth of children. This is an observed fact in the realm of the secondary consciousness. In the realm of our primary awareness of ourselves, it is experienced immediately as a blind passion and—what is far more important—as the way in which love for another person is physically expressed. The marriage act is or should be the incarnation of love, not indeed the full incarnation, since love seeks not only to hand on life but to enrich it and to make it more abundant. If the essence of family life is relationship then the childless married couple can and should grasp these opportunities for the good of each other. The fullness of the family situation is not theirs, but the essence is. They may extend their potential fatherhood and motherhood to others and although such relationships will have no biological expression there is no limit to their upward movement.

This brings us to the question of adoption. The work of psychologists has convinced us that the orphan or deprived child stands a far greater chance of healthy development if it is cared for by a family rather than by an institution, however well ordered. Adoptive parents are able to include the adopted child in their own mutual love, and if they adopt more than one, to provide much of the complete family situation which the children need for their full integration.

If the difficulties mentioned in a former chapter regarding the only child are valid, it seems that we can fully grasp the essential being of the family only where there are several children. The question of the limitation of births either by contraception or the use of the safe period is so important and has such a considerable bearing upon the nature of marital relations that it has been treated in a special chapter. For the present, certain facts inherent in the relations of different members of the family to one another will be briefly indicated. Before doing this the important and burning topic of housing and the places where our young people have to begin their life together must be considered. This is highly relevant to the whole purpose of this book. It is only too easy to look on housing as an administrative affair. This is a fatal error. Administration, finance—national, local and personal—have obviously a great deal to say in this matter, but the fundamental facts lie in the province of relationship. If these are neglected, the essence of the solution escapes us.

Le Corbusier defines a house as a machine for living in. We may disapprove of the word "machine", but the gist of the phrase seems true enough, provided always that we mean much more by "living" than working, eating and sleeping. We object to "machine" because it implies that a house is a kind of tool for use. It is much more than that. The human personality has a strange power of imprinting itself on inanimate things and giving them a kind of life of their own. A father or mother whose child is away from home will find it difficult to look at some object belonging to him, such as a shoe, without emotion. This is not sickly sentiment. It is rather that the shoe in some pathetic way seems a mute and silent witness to the absent one, and its witness is all the more poignant in that it cannot be uttered in words. The ancient idea of the *genius loci* is an extension of the same reality. The house is first and foremost a place where human destinies are worked out. It is not only for economic reasons that in many countries everything is done to make it possible for young married people to own their own houses. Ownership, like any other human thing, may be a cloak for self-love and pride of possession. It is far more often felt and appreciated as a guarantee of stability and permanence. Movement is in contrast to stillness, progress in contrast to absolute value. We become what we are. This is easier to do if there is a solid, unchanging background in the physical order, a home which is always there.

The house and all that is in it become for the parents and for the child a sacred place. One has only to stand outside a house in which one's family used to live, and to watch others, strangers to us, living in it, to feel a pang of grief and a sense of loss, even a hint of sacrilege. Those rooms saw us grow from infancy to manhood, heard the voices that we loved echo around them. Now as far as we are concerned they are silent. Something of ourselves is buried in that stillness.

The ownership of a house brings freedom from many external constraints and so would seem eminently desirable for the newly married. Yet the semi-nomadic existence of so many people today makes it impracticable for them to invest in a home of their own until much later in life. In a still larger number of cases, financial circumstances make it impossible. It is sad to find that the wealth of feeling and memory which gathers round the home has to be contained within the remover's van. Uprooting is a heartless business for young and old. The fact that we become accustomed to it is no recommendation, for habit here dulls the edge of sensibility and marks a real loss of the finer things of life.

It would, however, be absurd to limit the idea of "home" to a place or to its furnishings. Important though these are, they are only a background. It is the life lived within the house which makes it a home. All families develop a kind of unique ritual of existence. In a thousand apparently trifling ways and customs, the family establishes itself as an entity in its own right. Perhaps one of the most serious dangers presented by television is that it may cut across or even determine the evolution of this ritual. The resources of the family are enormous. The arts can and still do flourish in however simple and amateur a form in many homes. The family meal is still in its way a sacred banquet, although here the demands of work often make it impossible for all the members to sit around the table together even once a day. Conversation, reading, discussion, arguments and even rows, all these are part and parcel of our real growth and it is in the family circle that they are most genuine, vital and influential.

The family which is fully alive to itself and its own spirit welcomes others into the home. The value of hospitality for the developing personality of the child and its parent is immense. Through it we learn that we are not living in a closed society, an isolated cell having no connections with the outside world. We learn too that there are other family traditions, other rituals, as unique as our own, which may enrich ours and be enriched by it. Much is and must be taken for granted in our family relationships. We take short cuts. A wink is sufficient. But with those whom we entertain, a new ritual develops, the family finds itself acquiring a Persona, a face it presents to those who do not belong to it. We find that there are limits to what we can reveal to them of our own family existence. There are loyalties which not even the closest friendship can shake. The stability of place is after all only a symbol of the far deeper stability of the family itself. We belong, we have a habitation and a name. Our identity is rooted in the being of those to whom we are related by blood and still more by the love of son for parent, brother for sister, generation for generation. In them, we live and move and have our being, not a being which is shut in on itself, but which is open to an ever-widening pattern of relations with all those whom we come to love. The family is the school of love and of life *par excellence*. So much the more terrible are the tragedies which wreck it or divert it from its true vocation.

The relation of brother to sister is a union characterized by sexual differentiation but not based on the genital aspect of sexuality. In his sister, the brother sees the female sex in isolation from the complications arising from his genital urges. This experience helps him in his friendships with those outside the family. Friendships between men and women are always liable to make shipwreck on the rocks of passion. In the brother-sister relation, except in exceptional cases, this danger does not exist. In his sister, the brother becomes aware of female sexuality incarnated in a person with whom his relations are almost wholly intersubjective. There is little temptation to treat her as an object to be used or exploited. On the contrary, the brother will see to it that no one else deals with her in this fashion.

This purification is not a puritanical narrowing of the idea of sex, it is a form of relation in which the young man's own sexuality is preserved from the process of objectivization which is so dangerous for his own development. It should and often does affect his whole approach to other women. Not, it must be repeated, that it is possible to treat them as though they were his sisters. This would be to blind oneself to facts. It is rather that, having once seen sex in its subjective form, he is better able to make allowance for the pull of passion when he meets it outside the family. He is to that extent forewarned and forearmed. When he becomes conscious of the attraction and fascination of other women he is faced with the option of treating them as subjects in their own right or as objects for his pleasure. Shall he treat the sexuality of the woman he loves as a sacred sign of personality—as it so obviously is in his sister—or shall he look on it as a mere source of his own delight, a possession? This is not a question of the unhealthy suppression of his own genital impulses, but of their proper direction.

The special nature and significance of the brother-sister relationship stands out in sharper relief if compared with that of mother and son. This relation is steeped in mystery. It is so deeply rooted in the being of both persons that any attempt at an objective analysis inevitably fails in its purpose. The son is bound to the mother by ties which go down into the near and distant past, into the mysteries of human generation. The

mystery of existence and of the origins of personality are involved. We might even say the mystery of identity, since if a
child discovers that the woman he has always believed to be
his mother is not so in fact, he experiences a kind of plunge
into an abyss of nothingness. Who then am I? he will ask.
The sexuality of the mother cannot be an objective thing for
her son, for he is included in it. In her, therefore, he sees sex
as a source, an origin both of physical existence and of personality. This may lead him to expect that his future sexual relations with his wife will absorb him into her life in much the
same way as his filiation to his mother has involved him in
hers.

This mother-fixation, particularly if it is unconscious, is the
cause of many of the difficulties in early married life. The husband, whether or not he is aware of it, may try to recover,
in his relations with his wife, that security and enveloping
tenderness to which he was accustomed in his relation with
his mother. The wife may accept this role of mother-substitute
and little harm may appear to result until the first baby is
born. The husband may then grow jealous of it and so the
problem of his psychological weaning from his own mother,
which should have been faced long before, now arises once
more and causes severe strains and stresses in the married relationship. In families where there are strong brother and sister
relationships, there is less danger of all this. The brother will
have learned to accept women in a role other than that of
mother, and will have discovered that sexuality is not only a
source of life, but also a characteristic of being and of personality as such, and so is capable of influencing every aspect
of life.

The brother-sister relation is a school of pure loyalty, of
fidelity without passion. A man may remain faithful to his
wife out of fear of losing her. His loyalty to his sister cannot
be based on any such emotion. It is inscribed in his and her
being as members of the same family. This rocklike fidelity is

a preparation for an equally unswerving loyalty to the wife, although, in her case, loyalty will arise from a free act of choice, a total and willed engagement. So profoundly significant is the brother-sister relation that it goes far deeper than the public loyalties to the community and the nation. Sophocles has illustrated this fact for all time. In the tragedy of Antigone there is far more than a conflict between the command of the king, the public law on the one hand, and private duty on the other. The loyalty of Antigone to her brothers is rooted in the fact of her and their very being and is stronger than death. The loyalty of the subject to his prince has no such profound inscription in a man. The laws of the State, of first importance though they are, are—at least in their statutory form—the result of historical events, the creation of circumstances. The laws of family loyalty originate in a natural force, beneath and beyond the march of history.

The relations of the older children and the younger in a large family offer a very fruitful field of study. Here we can only indicate a few of the connections these relations have with the inevitable and necessary struggle of the generations. It is possible for the eldest child to be say, thirty-two years of age with a mother of fifty, whilst the youngest child is only a few weeks old. The time space between the mother's age and that of her eldest child is thus much smaller than that existing between this child and the baby of the family. In spite of this, the two children belong to the same generation; the mother belongs to another. Even when the age-span is not so extreme, there is therefore in the large family a bridge linking the generations which is highly significant, for the young child learns to separate the idea of adult status from that of father and mother. His older brothers and sisters probably will have already reached this status and may themselves be married. They and he are in the same generation-relation to their parents. They are all children of the same father and mother. The young ones become conscious of the fact that it is not time which separates one generation from another, but a special relation between parents and children. They are able to enjoy the love and care of persons considerably older than themselves, who are yet not divided from them by the genuine gulf of a different generation. This accustoms them from their earliest years to living with adults on an equal footing. It makes it possible for them to grow towards their own adulthood by a process of imitation which the parent-child relation makes difficult, because of the psychological stresses which are inseparable from it during childhood. Imitation of the parents there certainly is, but it is far more unconscious than imitation of brothers and sisters. It is for that reason much more powerful, a hidden force driving the young to attitudes which may be far from favourable to the growth of their own personalities. We shall say more of this in a moment. The elder members of the same generation exert a genuine educative influence on the younger ones. And this influence affects the whole attitude of both younger and older children towards relationships between adults and children as such. The large family does not or should not suffer from the disease of segregation. If it did, it could not survive.

There are crises in the development of relations between children of the same family. There are struggles for power, authority, property. There may be jealousy, particularly if parents show marked preference for one or other of the children. In this latter case, the role of the youngest has a unifying influence upon the rest. The baby of the family normally attracts all his elders and they tend to unite in his interests.

The novelist and dramatist have described time and time again the warfare between children of the same parents. Folklore and mythology are full of it. The concept of the family as an octopus, a knot of vipers, a den of cruelty and tyranny, is so common that the general public accepts it as an accurate account of an institution from which it is our duty to escape as soon as we can. The trouble is that conflicts about authority, power and property are the kind of experience which can be made public and come within the scope of a general or even a legal judgment. What is beyond the reach of the novelist is the essential unity and love between the members of a family. It is this sharing in love which is so difficult to describe. Only occasionally does a Mauriac succeed in suggesting its immense resonance, as in the last chapter of *Le Mystère Frontenac*.

Studies of the other relational patterns in the family would reveal the inner nature of that community and make us more fully aware of its primordial role in the unfolding of our personality, more fully aware too of what we owe to it and the obligations it places upon us. We can only offer here one or two lines of thought and research into five other elements in the family pattern—father and son, father and daughter, grandparents, sick members, the dead. We have purposely avoided such relationships as those of mother and daughter since they are obviously in themselves outside my experience, as a man, to describe. A man can only note their effects. He cannot enter subjectively into them.

The mention of father and son immediately brings to mind the equivocal figure of Oedipus, introduced into the realm of sexuality by Sigmund Freud. This is not a treatise on psychology. We can do no more than mention briefly what Freud taught and the modification suggested by Jung. This much we are bound to do, if only to avoid being accused of neglecting a theory which has had immense and not always happy consequences in recent years. On the solution of the Oedipus complex depends, in the view of Freud and his psycho-analytical school, the successful emergence of a truly balanced and adult emotional and even intellectual life. The essence of the doctrine is this—the child has to identify himself or herself with the parent of the same sex in order to become a true adult. The unconscious imitation of the parent and the great issues that hang upon it have already been mentioned. But according to Freud, the child—still unconsciously—attempts to assume the sexual role of the parent and so, in the case of the son, to impregnate the mother. This sexual assault is symbolized by various patterns of child behaviour. Once the child has identified himself with the parent, the complex is resolved, the unconscious urge to possess the parent of the other sex disappears and the healthy psychological development of the child is assured. Should the complex remain unresolved, a deep-seated sense of guilt will persist and give rise to symptoms of a neurotic or psychotic character.

As an explanation of neurosis, this theory has had a great success. I am not competent, nor is this the place, to criticize it. I now merely state the Jungian teaching and leave the reader to study the subject further if he so desires. For Jung, sex is the first differentiation of a single life-force. This primordial energy is canalized in sexuality, but as personality develops it moves into every department of emotional and intellectual life. The incest motive which Freud saw as dominating the child's unconscious is, in fact, not genuinely incestuous at all. The great issue at stake in childhood, and indeed throughout life, is the growth in each of us of that unique personality we are all destined to become. In order to achieve it, we constantly need to be reborn or, in the terms of Jungian analytical psychology, to go down into the unconscious and to find there the hidden aspects of our selves which the objective life, the life of the Persona, prevents us from realizing are even there. If there is an infantile incestuous urge, it is only itself a symbol of this constant call to return to the womb of the unconscious and there to discover the Self we are called to be.

This brief introduction to a vast and fascinating realm of thought and experience must suffice; though it must be added that, as will be seen in the next few paragraphs, the actual experiences of the son and the father reveal that the point at issue between them, whether they are aware of it or not, is the personality of each, and its challenge to that of the other.

The son, particularly in early childhood, is physically and mentally dependent on his father. This is a state from which he must emerge and the urge to do so very soon becomes apparent. The father, like Oedipus, is an equivocal figure. He is both a source and an obstacle, a necessity and an incubus. The relations of the son and the mother are at a very different level. However unconsciously, the son is still carried within the womb of her love and care, and love begets love. But the father is a much more external person. He is the foundation of the family's economic life, he is also the source of authority and rule. The son, too, is destined ultimately to the same role in another community of which he will one day be the head. How can he evolve towards this status here and now without conflict with the father who is set over him? He depends on him for his own personal evolution both negatively and positively. He must both co-operate and yet stand out against his father. Unconsciously and consciously, he imitates him, attempts to assert his own rights, to think and act for himself. But the father has his own position and duty both towards himself and the other members of the family. There is bound to be a head-on collision sooner or later.

The father, in Freudian language, is in a sense an incarnation of the Super-Ego, that complex web of habits, principles and prohibitions which stand in the way of the child's instinctive behaviour. If life is to be possible under such circumstances there must be some kind of compromise. It is here that the importance of the father's own personality is so great. If his authority is harsh, tyrannical, irrational, the child's conduct may indeed be exemplary, but it is based on an increasingly powerful fear. Anxiety presides over the choices he makes and he becomes the victim of a repression mechanism which will have grave consequences in later life. This does not mean that discipline is a bad thing or that a father must offer a reason for every order he gives to his son. Lack of discipline is almost as fatal as excess of it, and the child is not yet capable of understanding explanations which justify certain types of paternal command. The essential need is for him to feel that his father loves him and that anger or peremptoriness are not signs of hatred. The father-son situation is bound to be an uneasy one, but it is necessary. Without it, the son lacks that foundation of stability and authority which will enable him to acquire in time a mature and balanced personality.

This difficult period has to be lived through. There is no hope of taking a short cut. When the son is old enough to stand on his own feet, to control himself, when he has reached the stage at which he can see his father as a person and not merely as an authority, then relations of profound friendship and mutual understanding become possible. Some fathers try to adopt an "I'm your best pal, my son" attitude long before the child is ready for it. It is the son who has to find out for himself when such a relation is genuine. Boys have a sure and uncanny knack of seeing through pretence. They have no respect for a man—even if he is their father—who puts on an act and behaves in what they think is a boyish manner. A child expects and needs a manly attitude to life and relationships in his father. To refuse it to him only increases his anxieties.

There is a custom in some families which encourages the children to call parents by their Christian names. It seems pointless. The word "father" in the fullness of its meaning and implications is the most honourable title a man can receive and a child can use. To be able to give life and give it more abundantly, to be the origin and the educator of sons, is a sign of maturity and adult status. To call one's father "Bill" or "Harry" may appear a small thing, but it suggests a lack of respect for a great vocation, a lack of appreciation of the true grounds for our relationship with the man who begat us.

Where there is more than one son, the father will find that there is no single, stereotyped way of dealing with them all. This situation raises new problems. We are all familiar with the inferiority feeling a second son may develop in regard to his elder brother. Adults often add fuel to this inward flame by urging the younger child to imitate his brother, by comparing him unfavourably with the older boy in a misguided effort to spur him on to emulation. Teachers are very liable to inflict this form of mental torture on their pupils. This is not only cruel but useless. Many a boy has been prevented for years at a stretch from developing in his own way and along the line of his own gifts and talents, by this absurd urge to imitation. If the father falls into this trap, it is likely that the son will seek refuge from his stresses by depending too much on the love and affection of his mother, and his last state will be worse than the first. The great work of the mother is to give birth and to go on giving birth. She has, in the words of the Gospel, to "bring forth a man child into the world". If she draws him back into the womb of a spoiling, molley-coddling love, she is doing him a grave disservice.

At first sight, the reader may be appalled at the implications of family relationships and the vital issues that depend upon them. It is only too true that we tend to shut our eyes to them, to turn from them to the various forms of *divertissement* which our times provide. The issues remain and if they are not faced, lived through, grappled with in a spirit of responsibility and love, our children will enter the life of the community at large without the proper equipment they need if they are to be fully adult members of the nation and of the race. The family, the home, the parents, brothers and sisters, these are the primary and most important educative forces. Nothing can replace them. The family situations are those we need if we are to become persons. They are full of dangers and full of opportunities. They offer the real options of human life. In them, the vast implications of human sexuality are seen to go far beyond the genital mechanisms and the erotic experience which is all the word "sex" means to so many of our contemporaries.

The love of the father for his daughter is the fruit of the

genital love of husband and wife, yet it is—like the love of sister and brother—free from the genital urges. So pure an example is it of an entirely disinterested, selfless, outgoing love, so free from the upsurge of passion and the inevitable struggle against self-love which the marital relation involves, that we can think of few crimes so abominable as that of the violation of his daughter by a father. There is a sense in which the father sees in the daughter the wife who bore her, but now to be loved absolutely and wholly for what she is and not for what she gives. A genuine affection between a man and his daughter offers him still another chance to purify his sexuality from self-love, to assume Eros into Agape and if he can do this he learns, consciously or otherwise, to show and feel a new tenderness towards his wife, a new understanding of the depths of her personality, a new reverence for her as a woman.

It is no exaggeration to say that a daughter gradually learns to enter her vocation as a future mother through her relations with her father. There is an Antigone in every woman, the Antigone of the "Oedipus at Colonus". A daughter soon takes up a maternal attitude towards her father. We might even suggest that this is a sign of her maturity as a woman. Her first instinct, as she emerges from adolescence is to take her father, if he is worthy and sometimes even if he is not, as the model to which she will want her future husband to conform. There is a danger here which need not be laboured. No man can consent to be a mere imitation of another; in any case, this is to attempt the impossible. As the daughter's relations with her father develop, she senses that the type of friendship that grows up between father and son is not possible for her father and herself. Nor, obviously, is the relationship between husband and wife. The only possibility is that of what we may call a motherhood of service. This is difficult to describe. It is a unique relation. It combines a reverence for the father as the source of the daughter's being, a desire to supply for the mother whom the father has long since left and whose role he will not have imposed upon his wife. It is as though the daughter realizes that a man must always return from time to time to his maternal origins if he is to be "reborn" in the sense Jung has given to the term. The tenderness and the loving attention and service the daughter shows towards him supplies this need in a discreet and touching way. At the same time, the daughter herself is learning how she must watch over and cherish her future sons. This relationship is different from that of brother and sister. These are the same generation and although an elder sister often has to "mother" her younger brothers, the psychological and spiritual values are different in this case. The daughter is an extension, the right hand, of the mother. But in her relationships with her father, she does a duty only she can do and she is not a mere substitute for some other member of the family. Her sexuality too is here completely subordinated to the service of another. The value of this experience for her as wife and mother cannot be exaggerated.

There is a tranquillity, a stability, a lack of passion in the relations of grandparents to grandchildren which cannot in the nature of things be the case with the same children and their parents. There exists between the old people and the young a sympathy and a tacit understanding which would well repay more careful study. The inevitable conflict essential for the parents' and the children's generations is not repeated with that of the grandparents. The parents' contribution to the personal development of their children is like that of the sun, wind and rain in the case of the plants. The contribution of the grandparents is like that of the earth itself, silently supporting and nourishing the nascent life upon its surface.

Our own childhood seems more remote from us now than the early ages of mankind. The latter are known to us through our reading. They are objects which we can study. In the sphere of the secondary consciousness, things have a kind of immediacy absent from the former experiences of our primary consciousness. Historical time seems a very shallow and unreal dimension. What we may call "personal time" seems an immensity. In the case of our grandparents and ourselves, at least in childhood, deep calls unto deep. We have only recently emerged from the unconscious. They are about to return to it in so far as death will divide them from conscious this-world relationships. There is a bond of union between us which in a very real sense turns them into the Ancient of Days to our childish eyes. They became almost a figure of legend, an archetype containing the wisdom, the understanding, the peace of the unchangeable and infinite past.

This mysterious dimension, in which the relations of young children and their grandparents are set, gives to the early life of the former a depth of experience which roots them in the whole unfolding evolution of the race. The remoteness of the grandparents in the sphere of personal time gives to the unformed personality of the child a formation by which the historical process is incarnated in the relations between themselves and these old people so close and yet so far from them. Later, the more immediate fate of the grandparents comes to the fore. They are approaching death. They are liable to sickness and deformity. They live with their memories. The young man and woman will no longer find in them the magic of those earlier times. Greater issues than this are now rising above the horizon. Sickness and death are events which place the family in the presence of the ultimate mysteries, the most tragic questions. To these we must now turn.

Sickness is now largely a medical matter. We have built up a comprehensive system of hospitals, consultants, specialists, techniques of diagnosis and therapeutic methods. We have almost reached a point where a surgical operation confers respectability and has become a kind of qualification in the social sphere. The role of the hospital and the part played by the medical profession in our public and private lives are extensive and beneficial. Nevertheless, there is danger of our failing to see the real meaning of sickness in the field of personal and, above all, family relations. From a strictly medical, objective point of view, serious illness demands hospital treatment. From a personal, subjective point of view, to remove a man or woman from the love and care of his family at a time when his whole existence is threatened seems a strange thing to do. More than ever before, he needs the attention and the affection of those to whom he is most closely related, and it is of these that we deprive him. Some medical men, (for example, Dr Biot[1] and his followers) declare that there are many cases where, in spite of the lack of medical skill and equipment in the home, it is better for the patient and for his family that he should stay there. Healing is not only a physical process. The whole man is involved. It is not unknown for a sick person to lose his desire to go on living if he is removed to a hospital ward. "He didn't want to live any longer," as the ward sister quite often says, when announcing a patient's death to his friends.

No criticism of hospitals is intended, still less of the superb work they do and of the incomparable devotion of doctors and nurses. But I do emphasize that there is a problem here which does not receive enough attention. Our medieval ancestors were aware of it. Most of the work now done in the wards by nurses and orderlies—apart from specifically medical treatment—was left in their times to the relatives of the sick. We may not accept this as a solution. We must recognize that it was an attempt to deal with a genuine problem.

There is another danger also. In some cases, the life in the ward and the constant attention cause the sick man to regress to an almost infantile state of dependence. The hospital can and does become a kind of womb to which he returns. There is the further complication that, when the convalescent period

[1] *Le Corps et l'Âme*, Paris, 1938.

is reached, the patient is suddenly given back to his family and finds himself in a new and puzzling relation to its other members. In the ward, there was a genuine community life. He was one among many sufferers. At home, he is a semi-invalid, no longer the worker who goes out to his labour in the morning and comes home to rest in the evening. He is tempted to self-pity and self-centredness. To be the sick man in a healthy community is quite a different thing from being one sick man among many in a hospital ward.

These are difficulties which arise whenever there is serious illness. It does seem clear, however, that were it possible for the patient to face all of them in his own home, much mental suffering would be avoided. Sickness is a challenge to the family as a whole. By removing the patient to hospital, we take away a valuable function from the home. In many cases, it is obvious that there is nothing else we can conscientiously do. But the problem is there and needs far more consideration than it receives. Suffering is an experience which may enrich or decrease a man's spiritual stature. It may lead to an immense flowering of all that is best in him, or to an infantile selfishness. It is among those of his own kith and kin that he may hope to profit most by the trial he is called to endure.

It may seem odd that a book on sexuality should bring its chapter on the family to an end with the subject of death. I cannot agree. Death and life are the two poles of existence. The agonizing question of whether personal consciousness survives the death of the body has exercized men's minds since the beginning of human history. Nature, in Tennyson's words, is "so careful of the type" but so careless of the individual life. Is love merely a temporal affair or has it an eternal dimension? Is personal life the immovable background against which we must look on death or is it the other way round? In each family, this is no mere academic inquiry. A father, a mother, a brother and a sister dies. Where are they now? Or have they ceased utterly to exist? These are questions inscribed in our flesh and blood, in our love for those to whom we are most closely bound.

For the moment we only consider them from the point of view of family relationships. Later we must return to them, for we believe they are at the heart of many of the realities to which sexuality introduces us.

The child is not aware of death, but only of life. It comes to learn of death through objective experience. It sees others die or is told of their death. Death as such is not an experience of the primary consciousness, which knows only life, the life of the "I" and "thou". Death is not an object of the secondary consciousness, except as a phenomenon external to the self. We see others die, we do not experience death itself. We see its results, but we do not know what it is. Can we know it in the act of our own dying? If we continue to live in another sphere after the dissolution of the body, it is possible that we remember the experience of our own death. If we cease to exist at all at death, we are not there to experience it. It is the end of all our experience and so cannot itself be experienced. It is the annihilation of the experiencing subject. We cannot even say it is a state of absolute unconsciousness, for such a state is compatible with existence. Inanimate things are presumably absolutely unconscious, but they most certainly exist. If death is the annihilation of the experiencing "I", then it is existence, personal existence which is brought to nothingness.

When we stand around the grave of a father or a mother, when we say "Father is dead", what do we mean? We do not say "there is no father". We cannot, for we have no experience, no knowledge of an absolute non-existence. We mean only what it is possible for us to mean: "our father is no longer with us and we shall not see him again as we have known him". But we cannot call him nothing. Even if we say "he is no more", we do not and cannot mean that he is nothing, but only that he is no more with us. To us he remains "father". This does not prove that he is still indeed our father or that he is at all. It shows simply that the human mind cannot think of him as nothing, even though his body is dead. This is important enough for us to take note of it. We cannot brush it aside as mere wishful thinking. The inconceivability of nothingness is one of the staples of human thought.

I was once present at a talk given by an African. Before he began, he invoked the spirits of his ancestors and assured us that he was always aware of their presence. Only a narrow, objective view of personality and personal consciousness would treat such a conviction without respect. Life has come to us from our ancestors. We shall hand on this gift to our descendants. Is consciousness merely to be handed on intact from father to son, only to disappear utterly and forever with the death of the last human being? Man cannot sit quietly to this prospect. His most ancient burial rites witness to his belief that we go forward to further life. It may well be that, in the simple, pathetic furniture of a prehistoric tomb, we find the fundamental reason for man's hope in immortality. Is it not the love we bear to others rather than the love we have for ourselves which demands that there be a life to come? *"Toi, tu ne mourras pas"* is the cry of the lover to the loved one, says Marcel.

In Bede's *Ecclesiastical History*, a pagan is said to have described our existence as like that of a bird, flying into a lighted hall and returning again to the outer darkness from which it came. What better symbol of the objectivization of death or, for that matter, of life? But it is an entirely false account of our being. The bird was alive in the darkness, he is alive in the light, he is still alive when he returns to the darkness. We were not in darkness before we were conceived. We simply were not . . . yet. But we were alive in so far as we were potentially present in the lives of the long generations of our ancestors. In so far, too, as we carry within us the generations to come, they also exist in us. This does not merely mean that the dead are with us solely as memories, or that we shall live on only in the memory of our children. This photographic survival is purely metaphorical. To the family, the dead still live in a far more genuine way. They sat with us at table, they laughed and joked with us. They rose up and went out from among us. Their chair is empty, their voice is silent, yet they are with us, and with us by the very fact of their absence. The family group remains. The broken threads of life are soon picked up afresh. Yet the dead are with us. They have not left mere emptiness behind them. When we meet, the place they once held is still there. Though they are not in it, the very fact of its existence is a token of their presence in and among us. This is no proof of their personal survival as separate from the family existence. It only shows that we cannot conceive of them as absolutely absent, as mere nothingness.

VI

Divorce and Contraception

ANTHROPOLOGISTS USED to believe that, in the earliest ages of human history, sexuality was entirely promiscuous and polygamy the first attempt made to control instinct. This view is no longer tenable. The work of Westermarck and his successors seems to show that polygamy is a degeneration from a more primitive form of union between the sexes. It may appear odd that a chapter dealing with divorce should begin with this statement. Yet the principle of monogamy has to be considered in relation to the practice of polygamy, before the case for and against divorce is examined. If monogamy is an artificial construction placed by society as a barrier against natural promiscuity, divorce will appear as a mitigation, however inadequate, of an all but intolerable attack upon a natural instinct. If monogamy is the older, more natural form of sexual union, then the arguments for divorce can only be based upon the fact of hardship. Presuppositions arising from both views are present in the modern attitude to this question. The frequent marriages and divorce of certain film stars seem to arise solely from a more or less promiscuous tendency and it is only the legal framework of society which forces them to practice successive polygamy. On the other hand, the large number of second unions which succeed, where a former marriage has failed, may be cited as examples to justify a legal procedure which prevents a clandestine practice of what would in fact be a kind of virtual polygamy. In either

case, a further issue arises, the validity of society's jurisdiction, whether civil or ecclesiastical or both, over the
most personal and intimate form of human intercourse and
community.

If it is nature that has made us promiscuous, sexual codes,
personal, religious or social, are disciplinary measures introduced under cover of philosophical, political or theological
doctrines in the interests of the community at large, resisting
the inroads of an instinct that threatens to destroy the foundations of society. We are back with Freud and his Super-Ego,
but now the whole structure of society is one vast Super-Ego
preventing the promiscuous instinct from operating.

The connection between monogamy and contraception may
seem even less apparent. Yet, if polygamy, as Westermarck
shows, was introduced to solve certain economic and ethnical
problems, so too was contraception. In each case, the personal
relation between man and wife in the sexual act is subordinated to an important but extraneous condition. An
examination of the implications of polygamy may not be without value in assessing the arguments in favour of contraception, if only because the general use of contraceptives increases
a form of promiscuity among the unmarried. However laud-
able the intentions of those who advocate birth control by
these means in the case of the married, the methods they
advise cannot be confined to such restricted circles.

We are so accustomed in the West to the institution of
monogamous marriage that it is almost impossible for us to
appreciate the attitude of peoples who practise polygamy,
such as the Chinese and certain of the national African groups.
It is easy to recognize the attraction which women have for
men. We do not need to be told that it does not cease as though
by magic after marriage. Men may be said to be promiscuous
in so far as they constantly feel the force of this attraction,
whether or not they allow it to lead them to sexual intercourse with women other than their wives. The existence of

prostitution is evidence enough. Only a superficial analysis would call this general urge "promiscuity" in any but a metaphorical sense. Attraction in itself is a good and necessary thing. If it drives a man to intercourse with different women outside marriage, we have to ask what he is seeking in this type of union and what kind of union it is. The answers to these questions reveal not a true promiscuous, natural urge but rather a disease in the realm of human relationship. I return to this abnormality later in the chapter, for the moment it is necessary to distinguish legal polygamy from the casual unions we may be tempted to think of as its Western counterpart. They are nothing of the kind.

Legal polygamy institutes a relationship between a man and his wives as binding as that of a monogamous marriage. It would be wrong to consider such wives as mere prostitutes. They have the same general status as in the monogamous family. They are often devoted to their husband. The kind of life they lead together may have many advantages over that of the one wife in a monogamous union. Certain of the old arguments in favour of slavery—welfare, security, constant employment, care in old age—may be urged to justify polygamy. An even more impressive case can be made out to show that polygamy is a more effective bulwark against the encroachment of the State upon family life than monogamy. It presupposes a certain degree of wealth. It is a form of capitalism and as such has a greater chance of survival when faced with the powerful Welfare States of modern times, which out of the ruins of nineteenth century financial and industrial capitalism, are building a social organization so centralized and all-inclusive that the tiny unit of the monogamous family may well be reduced to impotence—if only by way of excessive taxation! The polygamous father may expect his large family eventually to increase the wealth of the community over which he presides. Certain passages in the Old Testament or study of the economic and social structure of some African tribal groups show clearly the solid realities behind arguments such as these.

I have mentioned the Old Testament, but what of the New? Does not our tradition of monogamy derive from the teaching of Christ and thus stand or fall according to whether we accept or reject that teaching? Ultimately, this may prove to be the case, but I part company with many writers here on one capital issue. I maintain that Christ's teaching on marriage is not the imposition of an exalted and impracticable code, but the restoration of marriage to its truly human and relational status.

It is well known that in polygamous households there is one wife who takes precedence over the others, either in her husband's affections or because of her superior status and domestic authority. In some cases or at certain times, these two forms of priority may be combined in the same person. On the other hand, it is likely that each of the wives will be called to share her husband's sexual life as and when his feelings determine. But some kind of precedence, even if only temporary and of short duration, is inevitable unless the man has no love whatever for any of the women and treats them all as mere slaves or casual prostitutes—a very unlikely state of affairs. Normally, he is forced by the situation to make some sort of choice. The personal significance of intercourse is present in his relations with some, if not all, of his wives. Polygamy therefore involves a measure of restraint and discrimination, a form of personal relationship. The sexual instinct is not allowed to act in an absolutely irrational and purely animal fashion.

Analytical psychology has a theory which seems relevant to the case of the polygamous husband. Jung believes the "libido" is simply undifferentiated psychic energy which, if it is to be available for the growth of the personal psyche towards complete selfhood, must undergo a long, complicated process of differentiation. If this does not occur, the psyche will remain dominated by the contents of the unconscious. Har-

monious development requires both an increasing consciousness and at the same time a constant interchange of activity
between this evolving consciousness and the unconscious
which contains the great sources of psychic energy. As
sexuality is only one, though the first in time, of the differentiations, it is clear that if it is allowed to control the conscious
—and polygamous unions may easily lead to this domination
—then other, equally important differentiations are prevented
from coming into existence. The energy is dammed up and
the complete evolution of the personality made more difficult.
If Jung is right when he says that the psyche is a self-regulat-
ing organism which, of its very nature, drives the conscious
ego, either through symbols or neurotic symptoms, towards
a complete series of psyche differentiations, towards a full
evolution of the psyche functions and a union of the
archetypal opposites, then the fact that monogamy has been
and is practised by so many races, suggests that the psyche
finds in it a way to health and happiness. This may seem to
press the Jungian doctrine too much in order to justify monogamy. We therefore say no more than that his psychology
appears to indicate that some restriction of the sexual impulse
is essential to psychic health. An entirely free and instinctive
sexuality would produce psychic disintegration and the unconscious would overwhelm the conscious mind, as it indeed
does in nymphomania and satyriasis.

Jung's delineation of the archetypes also has a direct bearing on the issues raised by polygamy. When two persons are
united in sexual intercourse there is much more involved than
the functioning of the sexual organs and the pleasure that
this affords. There is a bringing together of two psyches, limitless and inexhaustible in their hidden riches of energy and
possibilities of differentiation. However bestial the intercourse
may be during a drunken orgy, for instance—the psychical
relation is inseparable from physical union. The more conscious the partners are during the preliminary love-making,

the more vast and deep are the psychological repercussions of their intercourse. The Anima and Animus archetypes are present. These images of the other sex which we all bear within us affect the manner in which coitus is achieved. The man behaves, even if he does not realize it, in a feminine manner, and the woman in a masculine, at certain moments during the complex act they are accomplishing together. And, at the climax, there is a momentary but almost complete loss of consciousness. The great creative forces of universal life overwhelm for a few seconds the sense of personal existence. There seems to be no distinction of personality between the partners. They are one. The inevitable barriers that divide one person from another seem to be cast away and each personality lies open to all the reality of that of the other. The intense pleasure which accompanies full and mutual orgasm is partly if not wholly due to this sudden release from the limits of personal being. But it brings with it a psychological danger, that of the Anima projection. If the man projects on to the woman the image of his own femininity, she ceases to be for him another subject, a person in her own right. The whole relation has reverted to an unconscious Narcissism. Hence the absolute necessity of further love-making after orgasm. If this process of projection is constantly repeated, and this may occur in monogamous as well as polygamous marriages, the man becomes Anima-ridden.

Constant relations with a woman in all the other aspects of family life, an increase of the personal, unselfish, subjective love between man and wife, bring about the withdrawal of this projection and so release the energies it was withholding from conscious life. Without again attempting to press the evidence, I suggest that the monogamous union offers the best conditions for this to take place. It must be added that the still more fundamental archetype of the Self would also seem to demand the kind of relationship found only in monogamous union. If there is genuine love and a perfect physical and psychical union, the thought of such intercourse with another person is abhorrent. The infinite depths of one soul are sufficient to reveal the heights of evolution to which each of us is called in his journey to his own Self. To attempt this kind of union with more than one wife, far from leading us to still greater hopes, will only make superficial and egocentric a relation which is limitless in its possibilities. Here, I believe, lie the psychological roots of fidelity; fidelity itself is a primary datum of consciousness. Any recession from fidelity to one person in the sexual union is a regression towards a less conscious form of life and relationship.

If this is so, then the researches of the anthropologists, indicating that polygamy is primarily an economic and ethnical institution, would seem to justify the assertion that monogamy is the normal form of marriage considered as a union of *persons*. Polygamy is the rule in certain societies because the personal, inter-subjective relations are to some extent subordinated to those of the community, or to the desire for wealth, power and increased social status. The parallel between slavery and polygamy is valid. Both the slave and the wife in a polygamous union are degraded to the level of instruments. They may be treated humanely, cherished, even loved, but the essential flaw in the relationship remains. There is a profound sense in which it is always true that a full and genuine relationship between human beings can only be based on a fundamental equality of status. If a person is used as a means and not as an end, this equality is destroyed.

The possibility of establishing polygamy as a legal institution in Western countries has apparently been canvassed of recent years. There seems little chance of its advocates meeting with success. Our danger is surely that of extra-marital relations. These have only a superficial resemblance to those of polygamous marriage. They are essentially different. They are tolerated but have no legal status. They are held to be the private business of those concerned. Society at large does not interfere unless and until the divorce courts are called upon to dissolve a marriage and adultery is the ground for the petition. It may well be asked why "affairs" between men and women are not hindered by State legislation, while marriage is hedged about with legal enactments and administrative regulations. If the sexual relation is essentially one between persons, why has it to receive such public attention when it involves a marriage and none at all when it does not? Religious communions go even further. The Catholic Church, in particular, appears to assume dictatorial powers over the marriage bond. Is there any justification for this? Whatever our answer, one thing is obvious and relevant. State and Church are convinced that they have power over the marriage relations of their subjects or members. Why is this so?

The union of man and wife is precarious on many counts and subject to constant threats from within and from without. It cannot even begin, unless there is an undertaking on the part of both persons to maintain its stability, if only for a time. And such an undertaking seems impossible, given the hazards of human life. How can I promise to love and cherish a woman and to remain faithful to her when I have no idea how she or I will behave in the entirely new situation which our married union will inaugurate? The whole notion of a marriage vow looks absurd from this angle. Unless we each lay down conditions—such as the possibility of divorce if we cannot live happily together—we seem to be entering into a contract without any consideration. A contract of its very nature involves some sort of condition. How can marriage, in its contractual aspect, be exempt from conditions? Yet if, when the marriage contract is exchanged, there is genuine love, the two parties feel they cannot enter into their new relation if they are already, at the same time, making arrangements for its possible dissolution. There are indeed many marriages where the loophole of divorce is very much in the minds of the partners. Whether such unions are really based on love is more than doubtful. If love means what we take it to mean, any reservation of this kind vitiates the relation and bases it on fear rather than on mutual self-sacrifice.

So the married couple who intend to remain faithful for better, for worse, are conscious of their own weakness and insufficiency. They are also aware of the outside influences that will threaten to increase these defects in their own characters. They may well feel that safeguards are necessary. These they cannot themselves provide. They take the vows, but need help from without if they are to keep them. The mutual aid which they promise to one another requires a more secure foundation than their own unknown future feelings and dispositions. It is no wonder that this sense of personal inadequacy has led social groups, religious and civil, to support the marriage contract by legal sanctions of various kinds and, in the case of religion, to register the contract in the transcendental realm of the divine and to call down upon the couple the blessing and grace of superhuman powers. Whether this is a valid act is not the question; its existence seems an inevitable outcome of the immensity of the undertaking to which the married pledge themselves.

A similar chain of consequences is found if we look at the generative function of marriage. A woman needs some guarantee that she will not be deserted by her husband, especially when children are born. They will need the personal, economic and educational advantages which only a father can provide. Perfect love will see that they do not lack them. But is love ever perfect in this life? Do not the best of men feel tempted to revert to self-love when faced with obligations whose weight and permanence they genuinely had not foreseen? Must not a greater community intervene at such moments of crisis and insist that they must not be allowed to destroy the family?

To live through and profit by crises of this kind may well be the way to a higher and more conscious family life. A crisis is not always due to trouble within the family circle. Another man or woman may be trying to win the affection of the husband or the wife. Here again, perfect love would ride the storm, but where there is weakness the need for religious or civil safeguards is apparent. It is true that the efforts of Church and State to prevent the breakdown of family life have severe and necessary limitations. They can only act from outside, except in the case of the Catholic Church, which in the confessional has access to the inner conscience. Yet even here, there is no compulsion and the penitent has to tell his own story, which may or may not be perfectly true. Nor is he forced to confess. He has been taught what the results of neglecting this sacrament are likely to be. It is up to him to profit by it or to refuse its benefits. The family contains in itself the remedies for its own disorders and external authorities cannot take its place; they can only support it by legislation and ensure that the forces in the community which threaten the family are held in check. Hence the solemn public witnessing of the marriage contract by ministers of religion and the officials of the civil government. Hence, too, the laws against bigamy and, in more primitive communities, those against adultery.

The mention of adultery and the penalties it incurs in some social groups raises the problem of the attitude taken towards it in Western nations. It may be argued that the severe measures used against it in primitive societies are only necessary because adultery among them is a threat to the whole group. Laws against adultery are chiefly intended to protect society and not to contribute to the well-being of the individual family. They are the product of the group consciousness and, as such, inevitable in societies where, as it is claimed, the sense of individual personality and liberty is not yet highly developed and the family group, like the individual, is almost totally included in the life of the tribe. The evolution of self-consciousness in the more civilized nations, the broader concept of personal rights, have made it impossible for the State to intervene in the sexual life of the individual except when its own interests are threatened. Hence adultery only becomes of importance to the community when it is brought forward as a justification for divorce. This view seems also to be held by some religious groups, if in a more modified and less definite form. In our own country, there is a tendency in the State Church and among the nonconformist bodies to accept adultery as justifying divorce, although this conclusion is reached in a roundabout way. While disapproving of divorce itself, they will readmit to Communion on humanitarian grounds persons who have divorced their adulterous partners and then remarried. Thus tacitly they assume that the injured party may have a natural right to approach the civil courts without thereby denying a fundamental Christian principle: however much the fact is disguised under cover of Christian charity, and one has every sympathy with the state of mind which is anxious for the spiritual welfare of these unfortunate people, this assumption is implicit in that attitude. In the Catholic Church there is no question of permitting divorce in the civil sense with freedom to remarry, yet adultery is considered by the Canon Law as sufficient grounds for a legal separation. The Church claims no power over the marriage bond itself; separation cannot dissolve the bond.

Is the argument based on the evolution of personal freedom and a higher level of consciousness valid, and does it constitute a sufficient reason for allowing adultery to go unchecked as far as public authority is concerned? This is a difficult question. Any invasion of personal rights by the State is seen as a threat of tyranny and is rightly resisted. Nevertheless, assumptions which seem unwarranted do underlie the argument. If the State claims the right of regulating marriage contracts and registering them, at the same time refusing to take cognizance of adultery on the grounds that it is a purely private affair, then we are once more in the presence of a separation of the two essentially inseparable ends of marriage. The mutual aid, the personal relationship, is held to be beyond the State's jurisdiction, while the primary end, the procreation and education of children, being threatened by adultery, gives the State the right to regulate the initial contract. The State, in short, is only interested in the family as an institution and refuses to do anything to prevent that institution from foundering through an abuse of personal liberty on the part of either husband or wife. In cases where the State forbids divorce, this care for the institution and neglect of the persons who compose it are all the more apparent and hard to understand.

A cynic might say that public intervention in the one case and abstention in the other are due to the sexual habits of the middle classes, who have for so long controlled the states of Western Europe. The ruling classes are unwilling that the State should stop them from doing as they like in the matter of sexual intercourse, but they are only too glad, for economic, social and financial reasons, that the family as an institution should receive legal confirmation in the statute books. There is something in this argument. The two standards of conduct, one for men, the other for women, were a disagreeable feature of the nineteenth-century sexual code. But the fact remains that, for whatever reason, sexual intercourse as such is not considered to be within the sphere of public legislation. The direct result is the institution of the Divorce Courts. Their effect is twofold. They offer redress to the injured party and they make it possible for both partners to commit adultery with the object of achieving the end in view, that is the civil dissolution of their marriage. That increasingly large numbers of people are using the courts for this purpose and adultery as a means to divorce is only too obvious.

We cannot here examine all the implications of these facts, and confine ourselves to the case of a wife or husband who, unable to remain physically faithful, practices extra-marital intercourse solely because of this supposed inability to control the sexual instinct or, more tragically, because he or she has fallen in love with a third party. This means that we must try to find out why some married people indulge in casual sexual relations with prostitutes or, in the woman's case, with men willing to co-operate, while others form a liaison with a mistress or a lover. The two cases are not identical and need separate consideration.

We have already seen the obvious temptation to which men are exposed. If they have constantly to be on their guard lest the attraction of women should lead them to forget the demands of love and the rights of the human person, it seems odd that it is precisely in their public life that they have to meet this challenge. Some writers have gone so far as to declare that social life is a grave and continual threat to the marriage bond. A bleak doctrine this, though not without some foundation; but the truth is surely more complex and more subtle. Western society has become atomized. As Christopher Dawson has said, the modern nation consists of a "dust" of individuals in the presence of an omnipotent State. This atomization has serious repercussions upon consciousness. If it is true that marriage is the way to genuine and fruitful relationships not only with one person of the opposite sex but, by extension, with all other persons, then the married state is the one bulwark left against a total atomization of our relational life. At the same time, the breakdown of the larger family group has reduced the scope of the relationship in marriage to that of husband and wife, even to the exclusion of the children.

The philosophers of love have done a disservice to their own cause by separating the family as such from the conjugal union which they consider to be autonomous and unique. Immediately, therefore, that problems arise in the personal relations of man and wife—as they are bound to do—modern couples are more or less thrown on to the public stage. The ancient safeguards against adultery are no longer there. The

idea that happiness is the criterion of success in married
life has made adultery easier. The man seeks a prostitute to
comfort him after a quarrel at home. How does he find relief
in such company? There is more in his gesture than sheer
physical desperation and indulgence. Whether he knows it or
nor, whether he likes it or not, he enters into a real relation
with the prostitute and she with him. They are both persons.
Here lies the real problem of prostitution. A great cosmic
force involving vast currents of consciousness and deep movements in the unconscious, involving at least potentially the
possibility of new life, is used for a trivial self-regarding purpose. The intercourse itself cannot be trivial. For whatever
reason a man goes to a brothel, the fundamental urge which
drives him there is a hunger for a new form of relationship.
This may sound absurd. It is bound to do so in our objective
and atomized society yet it is, I believe, the plain truth. Just
as modern research is discovering the profound void in the
personality which the alcoholic tries to fill, symbolically, with
the aid of drink, so also it is coming to see a similar process
at work in the man who seeks pleasure in casual intercourse.

It is by no means uncommon to find a man, who has
hitherto been faithful to his wife, suddenly sleeping with a
prostitute, apparently for no other reason than a vivid
curiosity to discover whether intercourse with another woman
holds a new experience for him. This element of curiosity in
sexual passion is important and difficult to understand. It
appears on the face of it, to be no more than a physical urge,
an instinctive drive. It cannot be merely that. Pleasure is inseparable from a sense of release, a movement from a narrower
to a wider environment. It is probably this experience of
release which the man is unconsciously seeking. As the French
say, *sa femme ne lui suffit pas*. The reasons for this insufficiency
are worth investigation. It may be due to typological differences or, and this is more serious, a failure to achieve that
personal relationship whose riches are so vast that any temp-

tation to seek sexual pleasure elsewhere seems a petty and stupid distraction to be met only with a shrug of the shoulders. If the family is the school of social life, it is through its manifold experiences that we are admitted to the society of those outside it, not through mere curiosity. As in the case of brother and sister, we learn in the family circle how relations can be established between men and women which though inevitably based on sexual differentiations, can be free from all generative urges and acts.

The curiosity motive has its point. There must be relations of the kind we have just mentioned. The man who sleeps with a prostitute is mistaken when he thinks he is only satisfying a physical impulse. It is a profound need for relationship which is at the basis of his intercourse. It is the woman he wants, not just the sexual pleasure, even if he is not aware of the fact. The woman is a person, a mystery, a new realm of being. There are no prostitutes among the animals. The strange and sinister profession of the ancient temple prostitute did, in its own terrible way, bear witness to the God-given desire in all of us to know others and to be one with them. It is in their married state that husband and wife "know" one another. A man cannot know a woman thoroughly unless he intends to be the father of her children. Extra-marital coitus is doomed to failure for the ultimate purpose of sexuality in both its generative and mutual love aspects cannot be achieved. The fruit of such intercourse is bitter. It is a return to the narrow world of the ego, to the contemplation of one's own lonely image.

Does this mean that the wife is to monopolize the relational life of her husband? Are men to avoid the society of all other women and seek a wider horizon only in the company of one another? Is there nothing but the home and the club? Are there to be no friendships between men and women? Can we conceive of them as free from generative urges? If we can, how do they differ from friendships between man and man? These are far from being academic questions. It is by no means uncommon today to find a married man spending an evening with a woman friend or his wife spending hers with a man friend and in each case with the full knowledge and consent of the partner. Some of these friendships lead to adultery and divorce, others appear to be successful. What then are we to think of them? They are a new phenomenon. Formerly it was the general rule that men and women consorted with friends of their own sex. Is this new type of association healthy or is it another example of a false relationship heading for personal and social disaster? It is not easy to give an honest answer. Much depends on the individuals concerned. Yet one fact remains and there is no point in refusing to face it. Sexual differentiation implies the possibility of sexual union. A man and a woman alone together cannot fail to be conscious of this differentiation. When they are in a larger company this awareness is far less acute.

The segregation of the sexes, which was for long a feature of English society, has been followed by a move to the opposite extreme. We believe it is true to say that genuine and healthy relations between men and women can only develop in a more general group life. To meet in the family circle or in social gatherings of various kinds seems a more natural way of promoting comradeship between the sexes than the frequent *tête à tête* which, whether we like it or not, makes us conscious, and at times embarrassingly so, of our sexual differentiation.

Friendships of the more intimate kind often develop into irregular sexual unions. The woman becomes the man's mistress. In Continental countries, the mistress has a certain status. The word and all it implies is not considered respectable but it is used openly and frankly. The common English attitude to sex is more immature and sees something "wicked" and exciting in the word and the woman who bears it; there is a failure to realize that these liaisons present a serious personal and social problem. Too often they are regarded merely as an adolescent prank.

The serious "affair" in the case of a married man or woman is in fact a kind of polygamy. The status of the mistress, although not recognized in law, is that of a second wife in so far as her union is relatively permanent. This places her in an equivocal and unstable situation. Either she will become the legal wife if there is a divorce, or she will continue to depend solely on the man's continued affection for her. Her status implies matrimony and in a polygamous society would be legally regularized. She constitutes a grave threat, as things are, to the legal wife and the man's children. The whole system of family relations is in jeopardy. Her hold over the husband has all the disadvantages discussed in connection with polygamous marriage without the corresponding advantages found in that institution. She therefore offers a challenge to our society. Shall marriage cease to be the relational reality we believe it to be and sink to the less differentiated level of relationship which it occupies in polygamous communities or shall we press for legislation against the practice of adultery?

These issues raise the question of marriage as a contract and of the whole concept of fidelity. As already mentioned it seems beyond the power of the individual to take that leap into an unknown future which the marriage vow implies. The promise is officially registered by Church or State or by both. This means that the larger groups not only witness the contract but in some sense hold themselves responsible for seeing that it is carried out. The difficulties arising from this public undertaking have forced many governments to place divorce laws on their Statute books, and this has led to controversy between State and Church in regard to their respective jurisdictions in matrimonial cases.

A contract consists wholly or chiefly of a promise, or promises, legally binding. A promise is not binding in law if it does not satisfy certain requirements in its form or is given in return for a consideration. In what then does the marriage promise consist? What are the requirements of form? And in a contract which gives one person power and rights over the personality and the body of another we cannot limit these requirements to purely legal formulas. Does the possibility of a consideration enter into the marriage vow? Has the State or the Church the right to insist on requirements of form or on a consideration? Have the partners, the Church or the State the power to revoke the contract or to declare that it is revoked? In a word, is fidelity a personal or a public issue?

It is often said that the passage from status to contract is the criterion of free institutions. If this is so, then we may describe freedom as the power fully to assume an obligation. The married are not free if they set any limits to their acceptance of obligations. If the promise were made in the following form —"I promise to be a faithful husband until such time as I find it difficult to remain so or until such time as you commit adultery," then the obligation is limited. It is made to depend on future possible circumstances which, at the time the contract is made, reduce the power to engage oneself fully thereby. The contract is on a level with a property conveyance or a promise of services. We are back in the world of the second degree of relationship, in which the persons of the partners are treated as objects or property alienable at will. The reader may approve this definition of the matrimonial promise and argue that, human nature being what it is, we cannot expect anything better. If this is so, we are obliged to rank marriage far below true friendship and place it in a category similar to that of business transactions or employment agreements.

If the traditional Christian view is held, the promise has a transcendental character. In the form of the Catholic marriage service, the vow is a complete and final offering of the whole personality: "I take thee to be my wedded wife, to have and to hold from this day forward, for better for worse, for richer for poorer, in sickness and in health, until death do us part, and thereto I plight thee my troth." Is such a promise beyond

the power of man to keep? In legal language is it *ultra vires*?
Can relative beings such as ourselves undertake an obligation
which in a sense is absolute? What, in other words, are the
limits of human engagement? It has already been emphasized
that marriage, since it is concerned with the mystery of life,
cannot be properly discussed without reference to death. In
Marcel's words "suicide is always possible". Where it is a
deliberate choice of a will unconditioned by unconscious impulses, it is entirely human and impossible for the other
animals. The man who contemplates killing himself will
argue that his life is his to do what he likes with, up to and
including its destruction. He claims an absolute right over
it. Yet an essentially relative being cannot have an absolute
power over anything. Tyranny is seen as a sin against
humanity. So too is suicide, whether or not there is any survival after death. The man who takes his own life thereby
declares that the race offers him no chance of reaching the
third degree of relation, of achieving his own selfhood in
union with others. He may be driven to such desperate straits
by forces beyond his control and his sin may thus be only
material and his guilt mitigated. The inner direction of his
act is nevertheless the denial of all that makes human existence
what it is.

If this is so, it follows that our very existence is itself an
engagement. We are committed to life. The instinct of self-
preservation has more than a biological aim in the case of man.
It places him at every moment in a situation where he may
accept or refuse the gift of life. We are not consulted when we
are conceived. We cannot be consulted until we have become
self-conscious. Existence has always to be accepted, our
commitment to life hourly renewed. And surely a similar
form of engagement is involved in the marriage promise.
Sexual differentiation is at the root of all human relationships
whether with those of our own or of the opposite sex. Sexual
engagement in marriage or in the vocation of consecrated

virginity is the gateway to full development of the personality. If then a man can undertake to live, to refuse suicide, no matter what trials he has to face, he is equally able to take a vow of absolute fidelity in spite of all the subsequent difficulties that may make him regret having made his promise to a particular person. In short, man passes in a mysterious way beyond his own relative existence, not by claiming absolute power over his life, but by undertaking an unconditional obligation. Fidelity is at rock bottom an engagement to one's full and final self, even before we have reached that ultimate goal of all our personal evolution. If a man always has suicide at the back of his mind as a possible solution to his problems, he will never fully live at all. No difficulty will be genuinely faced since he is always involved, even if unconsciously, in a struggle between the will to live and the will to die. The crises of life are unable to lead to the fuller integration which is the fruit of accepting them and living through them with open eyes. The same regression takes place in marriage where the vow is conditional and divorce kept in reserve as a possible release from commitment. The self-giving without which there is no growth in personality is in reality absent at the very start, and the whole pattern of relations in the married state is shattered before it can assume a human shape. It is for this reason that the Catholic Church does not recognize as valid any marriage in which the parties expressly include the divorce condition in their contract.

An objection will at once be raised. We are doing precisely what we have so often criticized the modern world for attempting. We are looking at the situation objectively and taking no account of the personal experiences of those whose marriage has brought no joy, no real relationship, but only sorrow, pain, misery, suffering, tragedy. In all good faith, a woman marries a man and takes the vow with all its implications and without any reservations or conditions, tacit or expressed. On the morning after the consummation of the union, she wakes to find her husband has gone, never to return. All the philosophy and religion in the world will not persuade us that she is not entitled to divorce and to remarry when she meets an honorable man with whom she has every chance of reaching the full relation which marriage offers. Or again, a woman is bound for life to a drunkard who beats her, terrorizes the children and is constantly unfaithful. Another man offers her his home. She accepts. He is kind, considerate, treats the children as though they were his own. Shall she on the strength of a mere philosophical doctrine or an abstract religious principle, return to the misery from which she has been delivered? Is she not justified rather in petitioning for a divorce and marrying the man who loves both her and her children? In cases like these—and they are not uncommon—even those who hold the traditional view may argue that under such circumstances at least, divorce and remarriage should be allowed by law. It is no answer to reply that bad cases do not make good laws. Everybody admits this, but in the face of such misery, the arguments seem academic and irrelevant. To condemn a fellow-human being to a life of wretchedness, or to a martyrdom which only death can end, seems far more unjust than to run the risk that divorce legislation to solve these problems may be abused by unscrupulous persons for other and less worthy ends.

Before this formidable objection is faced, there is one point that must be made. By "divorce" we mean the dissolution of a marriage validly contracted and the conferring of a legal right to remarry. The State in making divorce possible in this sense assumes that the dissolution of an absolute personal engagement is within its competence. This is a grave assumption of power over the individual. The married, within the context of their mutual engagement, have the right to separate for a time or permanently if life together becomes intolerable. Here we are concerned only with the question of the right to remarry. It may seem special pleading to argue that a couple who separate and yet remain mentally and physically faithful to one another are fulfilling their engagement in the only way open to them and preserving the relation without which they cannot achieve their full status as human persons. Nevertheless, it is possible not only to argue theoretically in favour of this view, but instances can be given in which the struggle to remain faithful under such appalling circumstances have produced men and women of amazing strength of character. To say that such achievements are impossible to the married is to deny the immense resources of the human spirit.

To return to the objection itself: it can be dealt with only by outlining an analysis of the situation in which every married couple finds itself at the moment of the taking of the vow. What is the contract they enter into? However clear and unequivocal may be the words they pronounce, it is the sense in which they understand them which, from the personal point of view, determines the real nature of the contract. It is true that the sense in which the authority witnessing the contract understands its terms will alone be relevant if there is any attempt to terminate it legally and publicly. Yet, even here, the Catholic Church will interpret these terms in the light of evidence submitted under oath during the hearing of a petition for a declaration of nullity. If it is proved that there was a mental reservation which in the eyes of the Church invalidated the contract at the outset, then the union will never have been a marriage at all and this may be declared by the competent court.

Strictly speaking the contract, whatever the form of words, implies the giving of the whole person in the case of each partner. This personal gift is the essence of the commitment. A conveyance of physical rights alone would be little more than a contract to mutual masturbation. I repeat, the real question is whether this gift of the whole person with its past, present and future, is in any sense possible. If only the absolute can give itself perfectly and wholly and existentially the creature can only do so by way of the sign or the symbol. It is presumably for this reason that the Catholic marriage service takes the form of a symbolical offering expressed in words which imply that physical consummation will be both an act of bodily self-giving and also the symbol of the offering of the whole person. In the English rite, the bridegroom gives a ring and a silver coin to the bride and says, "With this ring I thee wed, with my body I thee worship, this gold and silver I thee give and with all my worldly goods I thee endow."

The gift of the body and of personal property is an act of "worship". The husband offers himself under these symbols at the altar of another's personality. The contract is at two levels, the physical symbolized by the body and the gold and silver, and the spiritual itself as symbolized by the physical offering. The material is only a veil for the spiritual. A genuine relation based on this kind of contract produces a new community. "I" and "thou" become "we". To break that relation, to destroy that community does not leave the two as they were before the marriage. It marks a regression of both personalities. The partners have vowed to become and to remain a "we-community" with all that this implies when that community is included in the cosmic stream of creation.

If such a contract is terminable during the lifetime of the parties, their bodies and souls are only means to assure mutual service and individual happiness. A true contract between persons at this level cannot be of this type. If fidelity ultimately implies a promise made to oneself, if the terms of the vow thus mean "I shall not allow myself to deny or to fail to carry out this undertaking", then no consideration, no condition can enter into the contract. To allow it to be reduced to the status of a property conveyance is to deny the fact that persons are not means but ends. Were this not so, the institution of slavery—to take an example from another field of relationship—would be morally justifiable.

If one of the partners has broken faith in any way, he or she has reduced his or her own personality to the level of a piece of property. Body and soul are at the mercy of a vice, a whim, a passion. If the other partner then transfers his or her personality to another union, he or she has also sunk to the same level. Unwelcome though they may be, we believe these are the facts of our human situation. That situation is so exalted that it may well be many of us wish it were more akin to that of the other animals. But all our regrets that this is not so will not change our situation. There is no return to the innocent, instinctive, non-personal life of the beasts.

Divorce does not really solve the problem of the partner who is wronged by the other, since it undermines the whole structure of fidelity upon which all human relations are built. And fidelity is an essential to the nation as it is to the married state and community, for fidelity is a commitment to life and all it means. The sufferings of husband or wife cannot be treated as different in kind from other forms of human pain and misery. The doctor who witnesses the agony of a man or woman suffering from a painful and incurable disease may do all he can to relieve the sufferer; he is not entitled to take the patient's life or to suggest that he commit suicide. Our contract with life is a personal one and based on the fact that it is not our property. "I am my body; I am not my life."
These are difficult doctrines, yet human life is an inheritance bringing with it grave obligations and tragic suffering. We dare not evade these by escape. The price we should pay would be the loss of part of our very selves. We regress towards that indifferentiation and anonymity which the evolution of the race always strives to transcend.

If society at large refused to countenance such regressive tendencies, if public morality in sexual matters were firmly founded on realities and not on sentiment, the whole climate of sexuality would be purged and the kind of tragedy we are discussing would be far less frequent. When a husband or wife has to endure the cruelty or the desertion of a partner, we should see to it that the lot of the innocent party should not be so wretched that he or she is obliged to seek refuge in the divorce courts. We are far from such a state of affairs. While public authority is interested in the parties at the time the contract is made and in its dissolution, public opinion has not hitherto tolerated any serious attempt to prevent the causes of divorce. The formation of Marriage Guidance Councils is a significant move in the right direction.

Many divorced persons find happiness and fulfilment in a second union. This is undeniable and seems to make short work of our contention that divorce is a regression. Yet happiness is no criterion of truth. The inhuman implications of our actions do not always affect our own lives, but they are bound to alter the lives of somebody, either in the present or the future. This is especially true in the case of marriage. The cosmic stream of creation may be polluted and, although those who pollute it may not appear to suffer any unpleasant consequences in terms of their immediate happiness, others will sooner or later be the victims of their subhumanity. "The sins of the fathers shall be visited on the children" is not the threat of a fierce tribal god, it is the statement of an observed fact. The final judgment on divorce should not be based only on the statistics of the happy unions it has made possible, but also on the countless numbers of lives it has indirectly ruined or frustrated.

The mention of our public duty towards the victims of an unhappy marriage brings us to the final point raised by the problem of divorce. What rights have Church and State in the matter of the marriage contract? If the contract is personal, it would seem that neither should have any jurisdiction over it. As social groups, they have no powers over the person. For many Christians, and particularly for Catholics, the Church is much more than a social group in the ordinary sense of the word. There is a sense in which this is also true of the State in so far as it is the duty of the community to safeguard and promote the interests of its members. For the moment it is merely pointed out that neither Church nor State in fact invade the personal sphere when the contract is made, although the State does so through the divorce courts, and so, on one view, assumes rights it does not possess. At the marriage ceremony, the civil and the ecclesiastical authorities are present as witnesses on behalf of the larger communities and in the interests of the parties themselves. They thus fortify and make more evident the solemn character of the personal commitments which are undertaken. It is obvious from what has already been said that I do not agree that either has the power to declare the contract revoked. They have no jurisdiction over the free and mutual self-giving of man and wife. If an unconditional vow of fidelity is fundamentally a commitment made to the Self by the Self, then only the direct authority of God can dispense from it. If the Christian religion is true, if human freedom is a sacred trust, then God will not so intervene, since to take away the consequences of an absolute vow would be virtually to deny the power of man to make it, to deny an essential quality of human freedom. This God will not do, for he would thus modify the nature of man and of human acts.

It has just been argued that the sufferings of the married cannot justify relief by way of divorce. The mystery of suffering is so profound and so much part of human life that legal enactments cannot hope to grapple with it. Only the great philosophies and religions can enter this dark realm. Medicine may bring relief and, in its preventive form, do much to decrease its incidence. It can neither wholly abolish it nor even begin to understand it. But medical and anatomical research have devised in scientific forms means to solve some of the problems that cause difficulties and suffering in married life. I refer to the discovery of the modern methods of contraception and the use of the rhythms of the infertile period. It is perhaps incorrect to father the contraceptive techniques on to the medical profession, but it is a fact that many practitioners do not hesitate to advise their use in cases where the the physical and mental well-being of the patient appear to justify it.

Contraception is so prevalent in English society and is accepted so easily as essential to our way of life and as a truly humanitarian solution of current problems, that a critical approach to it is doomed to failure from the start. To attack contraception, it will be urged, is to place doctrinaire considerations above the needs of human beings, it is one more attempt to enslave modern man to outmoded orthodoxies which the urgent modern problems in the personal, national and international spheres demand should be jettisoned once and for all. Contraception is commonly regarded as the solution to economic and social problems in family life, as the only answer to the threat of over-population and world starvation. Nevertheless, the reader is asked to treat this discussion as a responsible attempt to deal with a serious situation, to believe that the motives which cause him to advocate the use of contraceptives are respected here, though the opposing view is maintained as the only possible one. The truth is that to neglect the subjective and relational realities involved is to favour that totally objective view of human life which will eventually produce greater evils and more agonizing problems than those that, it is argued, contraception will solve or prevent. In reality, it seems that the relational implications of contraception are not given sufficient weight in the debate on its ethical status.

The first point to be made is that in intercourse of this type, the biological process is modified. Is this permissible? Scientific interventions in the ecology of animals and plants suggest that it is; whether such interventions will prove beneficial or not in the long run is not perhaps relevant. It is argued that we have surely the right to make mistakes and to profit by them, provided our mistakes do not destroy us and so make further learning impossible! The experiments of the biologist upon other living creatures make it only too easy for us to assume that we are justified in using similar methods with our own bodies. This is a reasonable assumption if the body is an object entirely under the domination of the mind. But if the body is something we *are*, not something we *have*, the situation is entirely different. We are back with the mystery of the being we call "I". If we are both body and spirit, the body must obey the laws of the spirit and the spirit must accept the laws of the body. Our state is one of uneasy incarnation. We do not make it easier, although we may make it temporarily more comfortable, by denying in theory or in practice the essential unity of soul and body in one person. At the moment of contraceptive intercourse, this unity is in practice denied. The generative biological functions of the body are taken out of their context in the cosmic stream of creation —at least virtually— and the love of the two persons is cut off from its roots in that universal process of generation. The whole edifice of human personality is shaken to its foundations. This is an existential fact, whether we like it or not and however valid the reasons for adopting contraceptive intercourse may appear to be. Souls and bodies are used as means not as ends. We cannot risk having a child. This may be a sound decision. There are times when it is the only decision that can be made. Its result should obviously be temporary or permanent abstention from intercourse. Yet this is no easy matter, as those who breezily invite the married to practise it should remember. If abstention is not to lead to all kinds of nervous and moral disorders, it can only be successfully undertaken where the personal union of the couple is so firmly established that they are able, in Freudian terms, to sublimate their sexuality in activities they can engage in together and which will absorb their energies and so prevent them from coming to fear, if not even to hate, each other. Small wonder that the contraceptive way commends itself to those who feel unable to attempt the high adventure of abstention based on self-sacrifice and some common "sublimating" task!

It is doubtless true that many honest men and women adopt contraception because they realize they are not cast in a heroic mould. They realize too, though in a less conscious manner, that heroism is not something that can be improvised to meet a situation which suddenly presents itself. The fact remains that to avoid a heroic decision they are forced by the logic of the contraceptive act to destroy or to jeopardize the essential unity of their own individual personalities and of the We-community which they form. Such a profound wound is bound to have repercussions in the physical order, repercussions which may cause suffering to the partners themselves and to future generations. As far as I know no research, for instance, has been done into the relation of contraceptive habits to mental and moral energy. In his book *Amour et Institution Familiale*[1] Père de Lestapis writes:

When fatherhood is tainted with Malthusianism—and by that I mean egoistical calculation—which urges love to close in on itself, then civilization tends to become degraded and to sink towards a fear of all things, a fear of over-production, a fear of overwork, a fear of enterprise. When, on the other hand, fatherhood is alive in the hearts of men, civilization again becomes creative and not merely in the creation of "human material".

Presumably Père de Lestapis is thinking of the decay of former empires whose vitality seems to have been drained away, in part at least, by sexual irregularities, including some form of birth prevention. It would be worth inquiring whether the social and economic difficulties of modern Eng-

[1] *op. cit.* p. 110.

land are also partly due to a weakening of the creative spirit resulting from the prevalence of contraceptive practices. This idea, which may seem extreme, nevertheless raises an important question; namely, what is the effect upon society as a whole of the refusal of many of its members to accept the full implications of their actions. An attitude of withdrawal from responsibility seems to me to follow naturally from a type of intercourse which severs the elements of the personality.

Whatever method is used, the aim is the same—to prevent the fertilization of the ovum. Whether such fertilization would result from normal intercourse is not known, but the partners are not prepared to take any risk. Fear presides at their coitus and determines its form, fear of the child, fear of new life. However justifiable that fear may be under certain circumstances, it remains true that the nature of the sexual act itself is seriously modified by this negative and inhibiting emotion. The love of husband and wife, far from receiving its proper symbolization in the marriage act, is itself contaminated by fear. Each partner virtually says to the other; "Your body is a danger to me. A child may be born. We dare not risk that. You must arrange that the danger is avoided. If you refuse, I shall not have intercourse with you." We are back at the second degree of relation where bodies, persons and objects are objects in the literal sense, that is, obstacles. We haggle and bargain over them.

It will be pointed out that there is as much love or even more between a husband and wife who use contraceptives as between those who do not, or that intercourse without contraception causes a still greater fear. In given cases, this may well be so. We are not awarding certificates of merit to deserving couples but are engaged in the more thankless and imperative task of trying to discover what contraceptive intercourse is in itself, what personal issues it involves, what deep movements it causes in the being of those who practise it. In normal coitus, love works according to its own rhythms. In contraceptive coitus, fear cuts across the sexual acts as an expression of self-giving. Husband and wife may be deeply in love with one another and on all other occasions symbolize their love in many ways. But we insist that it is precisely this that they do not and cannot do at the supreme moment of what should be total self-giving of soul and body in their entirety.

The objector may smile and say that if this is all that is wrong, his conscience is undisturbed. It is regrettable that fear should enter into marital relations, but it is better to have coitus with fear rather than no coitus at all. This raises the question as to how far contraceptive intercourse is genuine coitus. It is a sexual manifestation. So too are masturbation, homosexuality, sadism and masochism. Is contraceptive intercourse essentially a form of mutual masturbation? It would be unjust to answer "yes" categorically. Physically, it quite simply is, but the psychological situation is not the same as that of the adolescent masturbator. In one sense it is more healthy, since there may be real love between the partners. In another sense, it is less healthy. For the adolescent, the urge to masturbate is a sign of the challenge which life and freedom are offering his developing personality. The contraceptive couple are refusing—for reasons which may seem valid enough—to face a similar challenge in their family life. They are returning to a semi-adolescent form of sexual experience, but with no hope of finding in it a way out to greater freedom and a fuller life. They do not accept the challenge. They are called to make an act of faith in the great purposes of creation and in their fellow men as able and willing to help them in their parental vocation (how far then are we all guilty of encouraging contraception by our selfish individualism which refuses to see in every other person a neighbour to serve?). This act of faith they do not make. They divorce body and soul in their sexual intercourse. They begin to come together and then at the climax of intercourse, they fall apart in an individual pleasure divorced from the cosmic realities of their situation. They follow in the wake of Tristan and Isolda and are sterile and introverted. In so far as their intercourse is a negation of life they place it under the sign of death. They refuse the gift of life which they have received to the children their bodies potentially contain. Is it better to have this kind of coitus rather than none at all? Are not the dangers inherent in it as great if not greater than those facing the couple who decide to abstain altogether?

So far we seem to be arguing against those who deliberately have no children at all. Most people would agree that such couples are shirking the great tasks of marriage out of pure selfishness and that they are essentially parasites in the realm of sexual activity. But the majority of couples adopt contraception only for a time or at certain periods of their life together. They do not intend to refuse fatherhood and motherhood to one another. There can be no fundamental objection to the spacing of births, provided the parents are generous in their gift of life and think of the total welfare of their children rather than their own ease, provided that is, that they are not "planning" with the express intention of sparing themselves and their children the hazards and difficulties of a large family, which if they are faced and lived through are ideally the best means of ensuring a firm grip upon the realities of human existence. An unselfish, completely realistic attitude is essential. There is no particular virtue in producing long families for purely selfish ends or with a doctrinaire intention of crowing over those whose families are smaller. The general principle which is inherent in our sexuality, when untrammelled by intellectual or scientific scruples, is surely summed up in the words of Christ, "I have come that they may have life and have it more abundantly". We too, without presumption and in all reverence, can say this of ourselves as the parents and educators of our children. And by life we mean the full personal life which requires the interplay of individual personalities in a reasonably large and varied family circle and the ever increasing mutual love and respect of its members. And this in spite of, or rather because of the trials and troubles of every kind which the life of the family brings to all of us.

The real choice that faces those who, while giving life generously, yet find they must space their children's birth for sound, unselfish reasons, lies between abstinence and contraception. Abstinence, as we know, may lead either to disaster or to increased love and harmony. Everything depends on the quality of the love of husband and wife and on the degree of personal integration each has reached. The prevalence of chronic adolescence in our time, particularly in the sexual sphere, makes it difficult for most of us to abstain absolutely even for a short period. Under the circumstances, it is advisable to make use of the infertile period. There is a good deal of misunderstanding about this. It is argued that there is nothing to choose between it and contraception; those who use it have the same purpose in mind; the infertile period is neither more or less ethical than contraception.

To say that both means are directed to the same end is to obscure the issue. The ends which contraceptive couples have in mind may be quite legitimate. It is the means which we are questioning. Those who use the infertile period may do so for purely selfish reasons. In that case they are no more justified than their contraceptive neighbours. To use a lawful means for an unlawful purpose is as immoral as to use an unlawful means for a lawful end. The lawfulness and unlawfulness of the means do not and cannot determine the morality of the ends in view.

We are dealing with two separate questions. For our present purpose, we must assume that both couples are justified in "planning" their families. If the woman is of the type whose menstrual rhythms allow the use of the infertile period, intercourse during that period will be very unlikely to produce pregnancy. Fear is entirely or to a great extent absent from this union. Fear may indeed prompt the use of the infertile period but, in the actual performance of the marriage act, this fear has no place, while, in the case of the contraceptive couple, it determines the form that intercourse shall take. The users of the infertile period take advantage of a normal biological fact. They may do so for the wrong reason and so employ a lawful means for an unlawful end. Yet, even in this event, their intercourse is not an intervention to distort and frustrate a natural process. Coitus apart from fertilization is a powerful source of mutual harmony if it is a symbol of love and regard for the other's spiritual and physical needs. Contraceptive intercourse implies the belief that man has the right to separate love from its biological roots. And it is here maintained that this is to act against the nature of the human personality. There is a profound sense in which we must refuse to deny our animal nature, to submit it to a technique. In our sexual life, as well as in our religious experience, there comes a moment when we must consent with our whole mind and will to the conditions of our state. If we refuse to do so, the way to regression and disintegration, personal, national and racial, lies open.

What can be done to counteract what may well be one of the major evils of our time? Once contraception has gained a firm hold on a nation's sexual habits, it is exceedingly difficult to eradicate. In so far as economic and financial abuses are a contributory cause, a more just distribution of the national wealth may do something to cure the disease. Yet it is doubtful whether the most efficient Welfare State will do much in this direction. It is an attitude of mind towards the meaning of sex and of generation which lies at the basis of contraceptive habits. It is a hypnosis of the objective, a failure to realize what great personal issues are involved, which makes it so perilously easy for this abuse to be but another instance of "keeping up with the Joneses". In so far as fear is present, a fear ultimately of life and its immense responsibilities to the past, the present and the future, we must hope and pray that the spiritual forces in the national character will again lead people to face reality and so see this fraudulent evasion of the facts of human existence for the deadly and death-dealing evil which it is. Meanwhile, in our discussions, we need great charity and understanding. As in the case of divorce, it is only by entering generously into the real and tragic experiences and terrors of those who adopt the contraceptive habit, that we can help them to make fruitful contact with their own physical and spiritual nature and with that Self which they all have it in them to become, in spite of the threats and hazards of our journey through this mysterious world where death and life engage in "strange and awful strife". We must remain faithful to life, faithful to love.[1]

[1] The Catholic has to realize that once the grave human tragedy which contraception involves and symbolizes has been revealed the problem of the regulation of births still remains. In medieval times the social structure limited births by controlling marriages. Since the breakdown of feudalism and its long-lived remnants, the opposite has become the rule. Marriage is not controlled but births are. That there is need for limitation both in the cases of individuals and in that of vastly over-populated countries is arguable, if not on ethical at least on economic grounds. Where and when such an argument is genuinely unanswerable, Catholics have to face the issue. They see the use of mechanical contraceptives as an escape from the responsibilities of human existence, however excellent the motives of its practitioners. As Pius XII insisted, it is the duty of Catholic doctors to investigate thoroughly and scientifically the claims of the Ogino-Knaus method. It is for the moralist to decide under what conditions it can be used in a fully human and Christian manner in individual cases. They have to inquire how far the method produces an unhealthy, because one-track, obsession with "pleasure" techniques, how far, too, modern research into fertility proves that moderation is the most healthy way to limit the number of births.

The "population explosion" problem, it is held by many, is only soluble by contraceptive means (particularly the "pill" if and when a certainly safe one is produced and can be used). Yet, however objectively attractive these methods may seem to worried politicians and economists, the fundamental subjective objections remain valid.

VII

The Second Half of Life

As THE years pass, we are constantly involved in changing situations. The changes may be small or catastrophic. In either case they register within us. We may be unconscious of them, they may be invisible to others, but they will have altered, however slightly, the inner pattern of our lives. The great issue at stake is whether this pattern shall be that of a kaleidoscope, shaken into ever-moving shapes by the hand of circumstance, or whether it shall slowly group itself around some fixed centre to which it will be increasingly related and upon which it will increasingly depend for its unity and balance. The life together of man and wife, the birth of the children, offer opportunity for our life's pattern to grow into an integrated whole around some such centre. The continual evolution of family life, the constantly deepening and broadening relations within the family and without, produce crisis after crisis. Each of these is followed either by progress towards a higher degree of personal integration or a regression downwards into a state threatening disintegration.

If we take Jung's four functions—Thought, Feeling, Sensation, Intuition—and bear in mind that some persons are naturally introverted and others extroverted, we soon realize how vast a web of relationship our contact with others of varying types will produce. In the family where all the thousand and one possible situations have to be faced, we find innumerable possible opportunities for our little conscious Ego to give way to that Self which Jung teaches us is the goal of conscious life. If evolution is the response of physical and mental organisms to the demands of new situations, then for most of us the family is clearly the great way of personal development and integration.

At this point in the argument, we shall refer to the ancient Indian teaching regarding the four chief stages of life. We do so because to see familiar territory through the eyes of another (as in a painting) often makes us more aware of realities to which we have grown so accustomed that we no longer realize their depth of meaning. The Indian religions, whatever place they may eventually take in the history of theology, are immensely subtle and detailed psychologies. It is as such that we bring them forward here.

In Zimmer's book *The Philosophies of India*[1] the four stages of life are described in terms of the aims which we should have in mind while we are passing through them. In the first three aims there is nothing strange to the Western mind, but in the fourth lies a concept of the ultimate purpose of the others which may seem meaningless to the secularist and perhaps to the Christian a distortion of the truth. In the case of the married, it presents a challenge which we feel is well worth our consideration.

The first period is that of the student, the learner, the apprentice, the man who follows a leader who can instruct and train him in wisdom, knowledge and understanding of life, of others and of himself. The aim which gives purpose to this time of life is that of what the Indians call "material possessions", or in Western terms the achievement of a place and a function in society. The second stage is that of the householder. It is a time when we reach our maturity, marry, found a family and play our double role of father and worker. Pleasure and love are the forces which drive us forward during this period, not pleasure in the sense of *"divertissement"* but

[1] ed. J. Campbell, Routledge and Kegan Paul, 1952.

pleasure in our own personal relations with others within and outside the family. The third stage is that of "retirement to the forest for meditation". We begin to turn away from the great tasks of the high period of maturity. The sun is moving Westward and the evening of life is not far distant. Here we meet the aims of religion and morality, which have not been absent hitherto, but which now call us apart and bid us prepare to leave our home and to journey into a strange country. Finally, the fourth stage is that of redemption and spiritual release. Naked we came into this world and naked we must leave it. All our possessions, material and spiritual, must be left behind and we shall go alone into the presence of the Alone. In this last time of life, we are to aim at complete release from all that binds us to this world, and redemption from all that prevents us from pressing forward to our ultimate destiny.

In previous chapters we have written, however inadequately, of the first two stages. Here, we will consider only the last two—"retirement into the forest for meditation"—"redemption and release". There are moments in the life of most happily married couples when the sense of one's own individuality and destiny surges up into consciousness and fills the soul with a sense of isolation. The joys of family life, the outward and inner experiences of love of wife and children appear then to be what they really are in this world, passing, temporary, doomed to fade away at the moment of supreme loneliness, the hour of death. Hitherto, if all has gone well, we have found the way of integration. We have succeeded in achieving a balance between our public, professional life and that of our family. The Persona has ceased to be a mask behind which we hide our inner personality not only from others but also from ourselves. It has become a window through which the light of the developing Self shines out onto the world of people and of things. Our love, our relations with others, especially with our spouse and children, have given us the opportunity to develop this transparency of soul. Our increasing consciousness of other persons has only been possible at a great cost. It has meant tensions, constant acts of self-sacrifice, delicate and persistent attention to others' needs. There have been times of real conflict. By accepting and living through these crises, we have grown to full adulthood. We have resisted the temptation to bury our heads in the sands of amusement, the thousand forms of *"divertissement"* our civilization affords. We have avoided the divorce court which claims to dissolve the realities of a present misery in the rosy hopes of future happiness. We have learned that happiness is not necessarily tranquillity, that peace comes not from running away from the battle but by fighting it.

Now "in the midst of our life's journey" we are called to enter "the dark wood, where the straight way has vanished". Freud went so far as to suggest that in the later part of life the desire for death, for oblivion and rest, begins to overwhelm our former longing for pleasure and fulfilment. The poets have been aware of the tragedy, the ultimate sadness of our existence upon the earth and have written of the final death of every joy, the quiescence of all desire. To the Christian, the solemn thought of the passing of the shape of this world cannot be separated from the blessed hope of immortality. This hope is not a denial of the tragic reality of our human state. It sets it more sharply into focus as the only way in which life eternal can be achieved. "Unless the grain of wheat falleth into the ground and dieth, itself alone ..." No marriage finds its truest depths unless and until the sense of our personal isolation and our coming personal death is brought into our awareness.

We have suggested that the death to self which love demands, and the living in and with the personality of others which this death makes possible, are the inner realities of married love. When the children are born from and into this love of parents for one another, there is a further out-going from the Ego to the Self. Yet this is not enough. The love of others within the family circle leads to the love of those outside it, who are brought into the orbit of its radiance and warmth. Yet even this is not enough. Behind, beyond, beneath wife, children, friends, stands the other, the absolute self from which all being comes and to which it must return. Beneath each one of us are the everlasting arms of that love which made us and calls us to an eternal union with Itself. As the years pass, as middle age draws near, the shadows of Dante's dark forest—the *selva oscura*—begin to gather around us. This experience also is essential for our personal growth. It is essential too if we are to discover the ultimate meaning of marriage and parenthood. For, paradoxical though it may seem, we cannot love wife, children, friends, enough until we see them as creatures who cannot satisfy the ultimate longing of the soul. As sexuality is the symbol and sign of mutual love between man and wife, so is that mutual love itself the sign and symbol of the love of God and man.

We must beware of turning back when we reach the dark wood. We will be tempted to withdraw from our union in the We-community and to return to a mere selfish egoism. If we give way to this temptation, our sexuality will become a drug instead of a symbol of love. In the forest our little ego is to be destroyed for ever and the self to rise supreme over its puny ambitions. The sense of separation from those we love should not make us seek consolation in a narrow self-sufficiency or a return to self-centred lust. When our children grow up and leave us, there is a real danger that we may do just this. We have fulfilled our duty as parents. Our love has been fruitful. The harvest is gathered. What is there left for us to do? Let us each take up the threads of our individual lives where we dropped them at the time of our marriage. Let us each in our own way do the things we have always wanted to do, but have never had the opportunity to do in the rush of our everyday affairs. Such an attitude risks setting both husband and wife on a false trail. The chief peril of this period of life is ambition. The desire for power and glory, whether in the professional or spiritual sphere is always to be guarded against. The real vocation of middle age is that of wisdom. Wisdom can only come when the full sense of our creatureliness fills our immediate awareness. To take ourselves as absolute points of departure, to consider ourselves virtually as gods, this is the endemic sin of the race. Marriage, when its implications are fully seen and fully lived out, does much to save us from this self-absolutism, since so large a part of our life is shared and in the sharing we are revealed to our partner and to ourselves in all our weakness as well as in all our strength. To know our weakness is to experience that essential non-being of all relative existence, that void within us which is the mother of both terror and wisdom.

The sense of isolation, the fear that not even those who are nearest and dearest to us have really penetrated our souls and know us fully as we are, the fear too and the sudden thought that the person who has been united to us for so many years and through so many joys and sorrows is yet still unknown to us, the stark fact of the unfathomable mystery of the other's personality—all this drives us into the dark forest and prevents us from rejecting self-idolatry merely to replace it by idolatry of one's partner. For this can be done and with disastrous results. When the family or the married relationship is made to take the place of God, a burden is laid on it which it cannot possibly bear. As Plato says, unless love moves from the creature to the absolute and the abiding, to the supreme and utter Good, its whole upward movement is halted, and the longing which is at the origin of its first flight into the reality of "the other" strains itself to grasp within a creaturely world that final prize which is to be found only in the kingdom of God. Surely this is the meaning of Our Lord's saying—"If any man comes to me, without hating his father and mother and wife and children and brethren and sisters, yes, and his own life too, he can be no disciple of mine" (St Luke, 15 : 26).

During the years when the children have been growing up, there has been so much to do, life has been so full of immediate problems and ever-changing demands, that we have had little chance to explore the depths of one another's personalities. Husband and wife have been looking together at common objectives. They have had few opportunities to look at one another. There have been moments of such mutual revelation, but they have been rare and fleeting. There have been times too when our weaknesses have made life all but unbearable for one or both. But the children's interests, the joy of love as symbolized in our sexual life together, have cast a veil over the more sombre realities of our being. Love is truly said to be blind in the sense that when it first grips us, we see only our own image in the loved one; then, in the tasks of married life, the vision of the future which the children incarnate has made us in some degree blind to each other. And all the time, the great over-riding purpose of our love has dimmed our view of the immediate creaturely limits within which that purpose is achieved. Now comes the call to quiet, sincere contemplation of one another. Now we may at least learn fully to love one another as and for what we truly are with all our faults and imperfections. This demands a new and closer contact with the facts of human life. For if, when our children have gone from us, there is nothing for us to love but our two selves, then there will be no issue from the dark forest.

The reader may protest that we are painting an imaginary picture or using emotive words to force a consent which reason alone would refuse. Let him then observe for himself the reactions of those in middle age in the situation we believe is theirs. How often married couples who have been hitherto mutually faithful now grow apart! The husband takes a mistress, the wife a lover. Or, if physical fidelity is preserved, how often the man will plunge into some form of "public service" and the woman join her friends in a round of "good works". Such activities in themselves are admirable. Yet there are examples enough of their being entered into solely or principally to relieve the tedium of a life together which no longer affords pleasure or joy. Even the considerable physical changes—the climacteric of the wife and the lessening of sexual passion in the husband, influence the situation. There is clearly a threat of dissolution facing the We-community. There is also the promise of a still more profound mutual love and integration within a higher order of reality which has always been present but so far has inevitably remained in the background of awareness.

We believe that modern Western civilization has everything to learn in this matter of a deepening consciousness in middle age. Jung has shown that the psychological problems of this period of life and the neuroses to which they give rise stem from the unconscious contents of the personality which now clamour for admission into our immediate awareness. The symbol of the forest is apt, for although the trees hide the radiance of the sun they are rooted in the living soil and their summits rise into the light of day even though their branches prevent it from reaching the traveller beneath. As on the mountain of St John of the Cross, there is no road here. The customary ways of conscious life are replaced by trackless woodlands. The signposts of the past have vanished. We must seek and find our own path to the other side. And in the forest are strange creatures whom we have never seen before, though they have always been hidden within ourselves, hidden too in the vast mythology of the race, that store of primeval wisdom which our breezy rationalism has contemptuously dismissed as so many childish fairy tales! Our loneliness is peopled with mysterious beings with whom we must learn to accept kinship.

There is need then for a new and more realistic approach to the experiences of middle age in place of that nostalgic longing for perpetual youth which so often bedevils us, as it did Faust, in our pilgrimage from cradle to grave. There is need above all for a philosophy and a spirituality of the married state at this critical time of life. If it is accepted and lived through as a crisis which will lead to fuller conscious-ness and deeper integration, it will bring a new relationship between husband and wife, firmly based on the facts of their new situation. "Your young men shall see visions and your old men shall dream dreams," said the prophet Joel. Here as elsewhere, the Bible shows profound psychological insight. The entry to the second part of life should be a time of dreams, of inward vision. The ambitious man has at least realized that there are wider vistas than that of the family hearth. What he may fail to see is that the widest vistas of all are inseparable from that hearth. His home with its fire and its smoke rising into the air is in the heart of the dark forest. The mystery of God and his creatures, incarnate in his wife, sits opposite him in the light of the fire.

The reader may ask for a programme. There is no pro-gramme of vision. In any case the individual and unique per-sonalities of all of us make practical suggestions an imperti-nence. What is needed first of all is an awareness of the im-plications of middle age. The rest then has a chance to follow. We must begin by "meditating" on our individual and common destiny, by becoming conscious of it. Now is the time to seek together the goal of all living creatures. Either we are to decay, our work done, into nothingness, or we are to come to an abiding city. If to nothingness, there is nothing within either of us to keep us together except habit and the fear of change. We have lost all meaning and purpose. We are the dead generation. Let us silence despair in distractions and use what remains to us of our sexuality in sheer and fruitless pleasure. Why consider one another's needs, why try to build a new life together? There is no longer any foundation on which to build. Let us each go our own way and seek some satisfaction in the world of affairs, business and pleasure.

But if we are passing through the dark forest in order to reach that last climb onto the mountain of contemplation where consciousness will flower into the final awareness which leads us to the kingdom of everlasting knowledge and eternal joy, then our common life will give us a far deeper love, a far wider vision than any we have experienced in the past. At the physical level, sexual life will indeed have ceased to be capable of bearing its natural fruit in children, but it will remain as the sign and symbol of our new pattern of love. It will be more rarely active in intercourse, more free from passion, more tranquil, until the last days of our old age when it is no longer necessary, for our union will already have begun to exist in the realm of eternity towards which we are quickly moving as the things of this world pass away.

There are psychological parallels between the crisis of middle age and that of adolescence. As the youth goes through a period when he avoids the company of others, so there is a similar period in middle age when there is, or should be, a turning in upon one's self, a temporary rift between the married partners. As in adolescence this inward movement is the prelude to a fuller entry into the life of the community, so in middle age the time of loneliness and isolation is destined to bring about a final communion with "the other" both in and beyond the married state. This new communion, however, is very different from the entry of the young man into the life of the community. Introversion then gave way to that extroverted attitude which makes it possible for private, family and professional lives to be led to the best of a man's inherent ability. In middle age, communion between husband and wife is directed to a far wider community. The days of the active life are numbered. The parental and professional tasks will be left to younger men. We are called to a more complete detachment, to a vision beyond the figure of this world. Our contribution to the life of our family and of the community at large must be that of wisdom. If, before old age comes, we have not reached this stable tranquillity of wisdom, this contemplative enrichment of our own and others' lives, we have failed to fulfil our whole destiny upon the earth. Many of the tragedies and abnormalities which fill the casebook of the gerontologist are due to a failure to enter into that relationship with being which is symbolized by the journey through the dark forest.

The difficult inward quest is itself only a preparation for the fourth and final stage of human life. This, in Indian thought, is the *asrama* of the wandering beggar who has severed every tie of place and work and become a homeless wanderer at one with the eternal Self and with eyes for nothing else but this. At first sight, this image of old age seems infinitely remote from our Western habit of mind, or even from reality itself. Yet the grave problems of the aged, which are now increasingly to the fore, should give us pause. We hear so often that old people should be encouraged to remain active, we are so harrassed by the sheer necessity of finding them accommodation and providing them with the care and attention they require, that an attempt to understand what the Oriental philosophy is driving at may help us to discover more and more human solutions to the difficulties we now have to face. Not that we are advising a literal interpretation of the doctrine and inviting our old people to become mendicant wanderers! Our awareness of our own problems can be enriched by a cross fertilization of our own psychology with that of the Orient yet we must bear in mind that we of the West are stamped with the mark of our own Greek, Roman, Jewish and Christian ancestral traditions. In these too we shall find the wisdom we need. If we listen to the voice of our own deepest selves, if we cease to pin all our faith on a broad but shallow objectivity, we may well find the answers we seek in terms of our own inheritance.

In the last stage of life, the shadow of death falls ever longer upon the married couple. In the majority of cases, one will be taken and the other left. In all, the thought of the coming separation must always be below the immediate surface of everyday life. When the moment of parting comes, there is a true sense in which the partner who remains is "no longer linked to any exercise, no longer linked to any place". Life together has ceased and often enough the home they shared has to be abandoned. We are here facing not merely a situational but also a vital and relational problem. Throughout the previous stages, crises led to the development of personality and this is equally true of the crisis of death. To think of the difficulties merely as matters of welfare and accommodation is to blaspheme against the human spirit. Sociological issues are real enough and must be faced, but at their own level. Here again, we have everything to learn—or to relearn.

The approach to the last crisis—death—demands a supreme renunciation. Nature herself prepares us for it. The senses grow dim, the mind less agile, memory fades, the body becomes weaker and crippled with infirmity. There is a call to detachment from all that made our former life happy and full. Simeon expressed the vocation of extreme old age for all time in his cry as he took the infant Christ into his arms—

> Lord, let now Thy servant depart in peace, according to
> Thy word,
> For my eyes have seen Thy salvation, which Thou hast
> prepared before the face of all the nations,
> The light which shall be revealed unto the Gentiles,
> And the glory of Thy people, Israel.

Whoever has known an aged married couple living in union with each other has known what this final peace can be. There is no more need for words. The two souls, the two persons, have learned that the Word in Whom they were created has made all speech tautology. The hour is at hand

when one or the other will move away into that silence which
is the heart of speech, of poetry, of music, the silence of the
Creator in which the only Word that is spoken is the Eternal
Son.

> Dum medium silentium tenerent omnia, et nox in suo
>   cursu medium iter perageret; omnipotens sermo tuus,
> Domine, a regalibus sedibus venit. Alleluia.
> (*Antiphon of the Magnificat for the first Vespers of the
> Sunday within the Octave of the Nativity*).
> When all was wrapt in midnight silence and the night
>   was in the midst of its journey; Thy almighty Word,
>   O Lord,
> Came from Thy kingly Throne. Alleluia.

Now the end, the aim, the inner purpose of fatherhood and
motherhood is revealed to them. Their childbearing was a
symbol and sign of the generation of the Eternal Son by the
Eternal Father. Sign and symbol are now to disappear before
the blessed vision of that unutterable reality, the majesty of
the Trinitarian Family. This is the ultimate Being of which
their own, both as individual persons and as husband and
wife, was a created image in the world of time. Faith and hope
will fade. They have done their work. One thing alone remains
and forever; "the greatest of these is Love".

You have assumed, it may be objected, that there is a life
beyond the grave. If there is not, what you have just written
has no meaning. At this point, therefore, we must go more
deeply into that agonizing mystery of the existence and immortality of the human soul. As we have already said, to
consider love and to shut our eyes to death is to vitiate our
whole inquiry. This we cannot in conscience do.

Men have at all times refused to believe in absolute death.
Even if this refusal is unjustified and irrational, its existence
and universality need explanation. It may be the result of a

desire for personal survival, of a proud wish to be distinguished from the other animals, of a hankering to find an ultimate purpose in man's existence and consciousness. Yet, when we consider the immense suffering which has been the lot of the great majority of mankind, it would appear improbable that the prospect of annihilation should terrify us. The Epicurean was surely right. Sorrow and pain are harder to bear than death, even if death arouses a greater fear than pain in our moments of joy and well-being. Man desires release from anguish of soul and body. No, it is far more likely that belief in immortality springs from a sense that justice demands a recompense for all the sufferings of this life. Yet, even so, complete annihilation removes suffering. It can never have its way with us again. The idea of death as a dreamless sleep from which there is no awakening has fascinated many men; it appears to be a solution to all their problems and a fitting end to a life of sorrow.

There have long since been metaphysical arguments for the existence and immortality of the soul. Their weakness lies in the fact that they are based on the data of the secondary consciousness. The soul and its realm of experience are treated as objects whose existence can be demonstrated either by philosophical dialectics or—in our own scientific age—by experiments indicating the reality of extra-sensory perception. It will be more to our present purpose to ask what data we may find in our primary consciousness, in our individual awareness of ourselves and of others. We have said at the beginning of this book that we are not directly conscious of the major part of our bodies. Our awareness of objects—and these include our own body—depends initially upon sensory perception. The existence, as distinct from the perception of these objects is independent of our awareness of them. We are not immediately aware, for instance, of the atomic structure of matter, yet it is presumably a truth. The existence of the soul as an object is not therefore disproved by the mere fact that it lies beyond our immediate consciousness.

The child, as we have noted, passes from a stage of immersion in the objective world, to another at which he becomes conscious of his own individual existence and begins to use the word "I". This second degree of relation places him in a situation of quasi-absolute centrality from which he must later emerge into the third degree of inter-subjective reality and relation. Is the belief in the soul's existence the outcome of a partial fixation at the second degree, is it an attempt to make the "I" absolute, beyond time, beyond death? In reality, is man, like the rest of the world of living things, destined to vanish utterly? Is the belief in the existence and immortality of the soul a mere illusion or at best a desperate hope?

If so, there is a scandal to our awareness. We know that the body is not annihilated at death. Its components cease to be united in our physical structure but they are broken down into simpler, material entities. They do not disappear utterly. Nothing is annihilated. All is changed. The problem of human death is simply that of the survival of self-awareness. Is this self-awareness indissolubly linked to sensory perception, so that when the organs of sense disintegrate, self-awareness ceases altogether to exist? Absolute death would then be non-existent in the physical world and reserved only for human consciousness. This is a strange anomaly. Yet it may be urged that the other animals presumably die utterly or that final nothingness may engulf all creation. Why should we claim exemption? But is there not an unwarranted assumption here? Consciousness the animals may have—we do not know and possibly we never shall know—but there seems no evidence at all to justify our thinking that they are self-aware in the sense in which human beings are.

There is a far more serious objection against the doctrine of survival and it is based on the evolutionary theory. Man, it is said, has emerged from a state of animal unconsciousness and has achieved self-awareness. He cannot claim this achieve-

ment as an inalienable personal possession of which death cannot deprive him. Human consciousness will survive in the successive generations and be the portion of each individual, but
only for so long as his body lives. Even were we to accept the
notion that self-consciousness has emerged in us—and it is
not easy to demonstrate this scientifically or to verify it as a
hypothesis—we might still reply that the very fact of our
evolution at this level shows that in man there has always
been a latent force, a soul which was capable of attaining
self-consciousness, whereas such a power is presumably not at
work in the other animal species. The question really is not
so much, how has man become self-conscious, but rather,
does self-consciousness admit man to a metabiological realm
of being, does it make him different from the rest of the
animals? Or is it merely a phenomenon having no meaning or
purpose beyond itself? We possess self-awareness and that is
all there is to it. It alone of all living things vanishes at the
moment of death.

In spite of all this, man has always refused to believe that
death is the end of consciousness. This fact is an element in
his evolution and needs looking into. It is, of course, true that
—in civilized communities at least—there have always been
those who denied survival. They have done so against the
sense of the majority. Clearly this does not prove them wrong,
but it does make them the odd men out. They often use the
argument that it is our overweening pride that prompts us
to our belief. Such an explanation seems naïve in face of so
powerful and universal a trend. Is it not rather that—to use
Bergson's terminology—self-conscious beings are here and
now aware of living not only in a realm of clock-time but also
in one of duration. The child, significantly enough, is not only
not aware of death, he is also scarcely aware of time in its
clock form. Modern civilization with its objective precision
has made the life of the adult, at any rate in its public aspects,
subservient to the clock. The more contemplative, subjective

attitude to reality brings the experience of duration to the forefront of awareness.

Profound aesthetic pleasure before a fine building or a great picture, in the reading of a book or the hearing of a symphony, has the extraordinary effect of increasing simultaneously our general and our self-awareness, whilst releasing us from the sense of time passing. After this experience we return to the world of clock-time with a start of amazement and a feeling of anti-climax. Was not the world we have just left our real home? Is not the realm of measured moments only a land of exile? This is no argument for the existence or for the immortality of the soul. It is an indication of the kind of experience which has led men to believe in both.

We doubt whether any metaphysical reasoning can convince us of survival. Yet, the fact of the mind's powerlessness before this great question should not disturb us. As we have already seen, in the sphere of the primary consciousness resonance, not meaning, is the rule. All the words we use to signify experiences in that realm—love, life, goodness, truth—are equally beyond the grasp of a purely intellectual human dialectic. Indeed, there is no metaphysical proof of our own existence. Life is a word with no objective meaning, but with an immense resonance. It is strange but true that if we attempt to define living beings objectively, we are bound to say that they are things which *die*. We cannot in fact define them or the life by which they live in terms other than themselves. The fact that most men are aware of life not merely as something we lose, but as something in some way permanent in us even after the death of the body, whilst not constituting a proof that they are right does suggest that we cannot be content with brushing the belief aside as mere wishful thinking.

At this point, we ask the reader to allow us to drop the impersonal style of argument and to recount a personal experience which is relevant to the present matter and to the whole thesis of this book. Some time ago, I suffered from a serious illness. In the ward there were frequent deaths among the patients. I lay awake one night listening to the groaning of a man a few beds away. Then suddenly he was silent. Those watching at the bedside went out and the curtains were drawn while the nurses washed the dead body. This sudden passing from life to death defeated the imagination. Then it became a frequent event and I thought I had become used to it. But on the day I was discharged, I realized that these experiences had profoundly effected my awareness. I had looked forward to seeing the streets again and the people on their lawful occasions. I had not reckoned with the fact that I myself had been at the point of death. All these familiar sights seemed unreal, tenuous, dreamlike. In the weeks and months which followed, this sense of the unreality of phenomena was to grow more acute and more terrifying. At first it took the form of a felt contrast between the enduring universe and the brevity of human life. Then it drove the point of its anguish into myself. The life that was brief was not some general thing, it was my own. It was not what I saw around me that was unreal, it was myself.

The reader may object that I am doing no more than describing the unhealthy imaginings of an overwrought mind and that this has nothing to do with the subject matter of this book. I would reply that it is during such periods of mental suffering that the separation of a man's soul from the deepest sources of its being is made painfully obvious to him. Such staggering blows reveal to him reality as something towards which he must strive. In the course of what we call "normal" life, the thousand and one distractions protect us, in the words of Le Senne, "against that anxiety which is the very source of philosophy". Whilst I was busy at my professional duties, I could enjoy life as a series of objective experiences giving pleasure, joy, problems and sufferings too. The problems could be solved by thought, the sufferings endured with fortitude.

But now, in the darkness, life and death were not just pieces in
a game of chess which I was playing. I was myself one of the
pawns upon the board, to be moved by unknown forces engaged in a cosmic struggle. I knew what the words of the
great hymn meant—

> When in strange and awful strife
> Met together death and life;

Nor was I alone, even if I felt as if I were. All men were involved in this struggle. It was not only myself who was to
go down into nothingness. All those I loved were also doomed.
Was our family life then a mere chance meeting in an ocean
of nothingness of a few survivors on the raft of consciousness?
Were we only waiting for the sea to overwhelm us in our turn
and utterly destroy everything that was human in us? Far
from being remote from the matter of this book, these
experiences are at the heart of the whole mystery of love and
relation.

As I look back at this terror of death, this threat of annihilation hanging over all those I loved, I now see that its immediate effect was to cut me off then and there from their
full companionship. Death had become an object, an obstacle,
the greatest obstacle of all. It had blotted out all that I considered meaningful in life. If life were a mere interlude, if
from nothingness we come and to nothingness return, then
this brief encounter with other persons and the universe of
things, this short interval of consciousness, was a mockery.
There was no purpose, no end to which "the whole creation
moved".

When the darkness passed, I saw that death and life were not
objects, obstacles outside of me barring my path to the hearts
and the love of others. They were within me, as in a subject.
I could grasp that death was *an* end, but how could it be *the*
end, the absolute end of all that had been called by my name,

of all that was I? No man has ever had any experience of an absolute end. All the things which he sees coming to an end only do so relatively. The day ends but is followed by night, the symphony ends but is followed by silence, the play ends but the lights go up. An absolute end is beyond our conception and imagination. Men who believe that death brings consciousness to such an end could not, I felt, have faced the here and now implications of their creed. I had experienced the anguish of the void, I knew that it separated me during my lifetime from family, friends, the universe. I was an outcast at my own hearth, a ghost at my own table. All reality, all beauty, all sense of belonging were destroyed. I knew what it was to be dead and alive at one and the same moment. I knew—and this was my salvation—that the void was within myself, that I both was and was not. If I centred all my consciousness upon the nothingness in myself, life itself would become impossible. That nothingness and the anguish it aroused were to be the place from which a man leapt upward into himself, into the realm of utter being to which he really belonged. I understood how it was that men fascinated by the non-being within them could lose their reason, could take their own lives. One could adore that nothingness to the point of believing one was the master of one's own life. It was a mere question of the formula O + O = O. No, if life, reason, knowledge, science, all human activity of mind and body were to go on in me and in others, the belief in the survival of consciousness was a sheer necessity. Consciousness itself could not survive even in this life without that fundamental hope. If love transcends the body, though symbolized in bodily acts, then there was no reason to suppose that the disintegration of the symbol meant the utter annihilation of what was symbolized. If love and life were ultimately one reality, then I could sing the rest of the great verse—

> *Dux vitae mortuus*
> *Regnat vivus*

The King of Life has died
And is, and reigns, alive.

The fear of death, once we have felt it within us, meant no more than the *"vertige"* before the sight of our own nothingness. But being is as real as non-being and I am compounded of both. Can physical death then sever me from all my relations both with being and not-being? Can it be an absolute end of all self-awareness? Is it an absolute in itself? Is it the real core of selfhood? If my relations with others and with myself are no more than biological phenomena, yes. If they do not transcend the biological, if my being is merely an object, yes. But if the biological itself is the symbol and sign in man of metabiological relations, if self-consciousness is a realm in which I live, not merely a bubble on the surface of the body, then the answer is no. My death is an event in my life, the external symbol of my confrontation with all in me that is relative, all that is not-being. Yet not-being is itself inconceivable apart from being. Why then should the dissolution of the body involve the total annihilation of all the being within me? Might it not be the other way round? Might not physical death be the final assumption of my nothingness into my true and abiding self? Could I not say with Christ and without blasphemy "I am resurrection and life".

Not that any of these considerations constituted a proof. Yet, apart from the data of revealed religion, this possibility seemed as likely to be true as its opposite. It had the advantage of making a true, full life of relationship with others and with myself feasible. If death were an absolute end, either suicide or a life of distraction in which people and things were treated as mere objects of physical and mental pleasure would seem the only ways open to an honest man. I could feel no sympathy with the view that goodness, kindness, brotherly love were values in themselves apart from being. If all men were ultimately nothing, love and friendship were nothing too. I saw that I could only avoid the darkness of despair and the terror of loneliness either by accepting life and other people as the source and means of growth of my own being and so, in their degree, steps to the Absolute without which being itself in non-existent, or I must treat life as a game and all its manifestations as counters with which I could play until the time came for eternal sleep.